Skateboarding is more than pushing around a slab of wood on four wheels. With Tom Cuthbertson, slide and glide through all the ins and outs of the fantastic personal sport that makes sense of smooth pavement.

Scott Sommers at the Pit

ANYBODY'S SKATEBOARD BOOK

written by Tom Cuthbertson

illustrated by Rick Morrall

photographs by Gary Niblock
Progressive Message

BANTAM BOOKS · TORONTO · NEW YORK · LONDON

This low-priced Bantam Book
has been completely reset in a type face
designed for easy reading, and was printed
from new plates. It contains the complete
text of the original hard-cover edition.
NOT ONE WORD HAS BEEN OMITTED.

RLI: $\dfrac{\text{VLM 6 (VLR 6–8)}}{\text{IL 5+}}$

ANYBODY'S SKATEBOARD BOOK
*A Bantam Book / published by arrangement with
Ten Speed Press*

PRINTING HISTORY
*Ten Speed Press published 1976
Bantam edition / November 1976
2nd printing ...... April 1977*

ISBN 0-553-10485-3

Published simultaneously in the United States and Canada

PRINTED IN THE UNITED STATES OF AMERICA

0 9 8 7 6 5 4 3 2

This book is dedicated to
Danny, Ray, and Thomas Zehrung,
who got me back into it all.

Preface to Bantam edition

Since the time of the writing of the first edition of this book (published by Ten Speed Press), there have been a number of changes in the fast-growing world of skateboards, and new and different types of equipment have come to my attention. There have been some changes and additions made for the Bantam edition to update the material and make it more complete and informative.

Acknowledgments

Special thanks to Mike Mitchell, Jay Sherman, and Rich Novak, and to these among the many others who taught and helped me so much along the way; David Dominy, Bob Moore, Shawn O'Callahan, Wayne Bassano, Bryan and Janet Loehr, Tim Vilsack, Tom Sims, Terry Brown, Scott Sommers, John Hudson, Tim Piumarta, Tony Carter, John Krisik, the Team Santa Cruz, Kurt Reynolds, Karrie Reynolds, Kevin Thornber, Laurie Karl Schmidtke, Phil Shipley, Roland Robertson, Gallery 115, Jim Gordon.

Contents

Introduction

They covered up the riverbeds with cement. Yes, then they paved paradise and a lot of other empty lots for parking. They put cement-coated holes in backyards for swimming pools, too, and they made a lot of what was left of the country into twelve lane freeways, one lane driveways, and winding dead-end subdivision streets with names like Parkwood Lane.

Yeah, they've made so many Parkwood Lanes it's hard to find any woods to make parks out of any more. Mostly, all you see is cement and asphalt.

The question is, what can you do with all that pavement, especially if you're too young or too poor to get a car and drive around on it?

You can gripe about it, call it unnatural, and try to put a STOP to it. But griping is a pain, and it's too late to stop the paving that's already been done, and besides, there's so much of it, it almost seems *natural*. I mean, it is now a natural tendency among many normal men to want to cover everything in sight with this smooth hard stuff that they don't have to water or pull weeds out of. Heck, these men say, if you want the natural look, all you have to do is paint your cement green!

That's how far it has gone. So we have come to be surrounded by a smooth-banked, well-drained, rock-hard environment, as a direct result of man's "natural" desire to pave over nature.

And what an environment! When the sun is out, it bakes; it raises the temperature of the air about twenty degrees, causes inversion layers, creates weird thermal mirages, and promotes general grouchiness on the part of the people who are trapped in it.

But what's that over there? What's that little spider-like figure wavering out of a mirage, spinning down the steep side of a distant cement culvert, dancing through a slalom of drain-holes, scaling another shimmering face, cranking a radical, gravity-defying turn off a lip, then shooting out of sight?

It's a little kid!

He has figured out what to do with all that cement.

He is using it as a huge stage for a rolling ballet, which he performs to the whooshing accompaniment of the wheels of his skateboard. He is in tune, not only with his skateboard, but with all that cement. And if we get closer we can see a pleasant, dreamy look on his face, a look of rapt concentration; he doesn't look like he is stifled or trapped by his paved surroundings at all. He looks like he is indulging in a happy fantasy. And in defiance of all the concrete, he is living out this fantasy. It may seem illogical, but actually, if there is one thing that is *certainly* more natural to man than paving over nature, it is indulging in a happy fantasy in the midst of unnatural surroundings. That kid, pirouetting through the culvert, is really on to something. He's found that it's *fun* to master all that pavement, if you pretend you're at the Bonzai Pipeline, instead of at the mouth of a city storm drain. He has discovered the thrill you can get carving big juicy turns down deserted hilly roads, imagining that you're at Innsbruck, instead of up at the end of Parkwood Lane. He's a pretty smart kid.

This book was written to help kids of all ages discover the kicks they can get out of skateboarding, and to help them do their discovering with a minimum of painful body blows from the pavement.

It starts with a section for the newcomer, who is perhaps a bit too short on experience and/or cash to take on the hotshot skateboards and the dangerous skating spots. There are chapters on choosing or making a simple board to start out with, and an extensive course on how to explore the use of the chosen board safely and with pleasure right from the start.

Then there are chapters on specially adapted techniques and equipment for each of the more advanced schools of skateboarding; downhill riding, flatland free-style tricks, and radical riding on weird terrain. Finally, there is a section on the history of the sport, written in an effort to clarify some curious misconceptions about skateboarding.

The book should enable anybody to get into a type of skateboarding that he can really go for. But the dream of it all, the fantasy that elevates skateboarding far beyond the mere passage of urethane over cement, that's up to you. For some indication of what this dream can be, look at the photographs included; you'll get the idea.

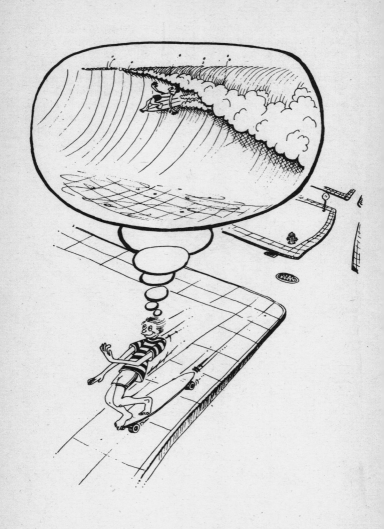

PART 1
Starting Out Right

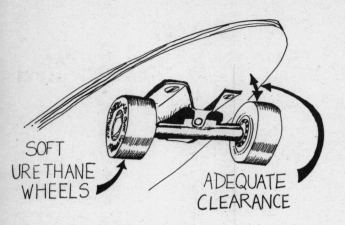

SOFT URETHANE WHEELS

ADEQUATE CLEARANCE

Simple but Reliable Boards

Cheapo Boards

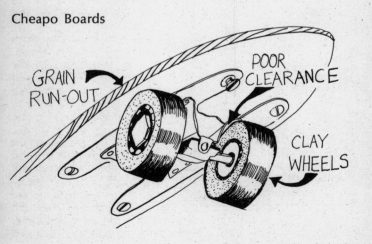

GRAIN RUN-OUT

POOR CLEARANCE

CLAY WHEELS

illustration **1** Boards with Single-action Trucks

1
Your First Skateboard

If you are a newcomer to skateboarding, you may be dazzled and a little confused by the vast array of different skateboard tops, trucks, and wheels that are advertised in the skateboarding and surfing magazines and displayed at your local toy or sport shop. The best way to find the right equipment for your own needs is to start by looking at the boards that are simple, reliable, and as inexpensive as possible. Work up to the fancy machinery as your style and ability get more refined and perfected.

The least expensive ready-made boards are mostly small ones (18 to 24 inches long) with single-action trucks. Although the trucks aren't adjustable, and although the boards ride a little differently than the more complicated ones, some of the simple skateboards are quite reliable and fun to ride, especially if you aren't too big for them. When shopping for an inexpensive board, look for one with good wheel clearance and soft rubber cushions, as on the Super Surfer and Motoboard single action trucks. You should be able to pivot the wheels a good deal if you work them hard with your hands; this will mean that you'll be able to turn the board fairly easily while riding it. Check the wheels to see if they are made of good soft urethane, and to see if they roll smoothly on their bearings. The new pavement-gripping, smooth-rolling urethane wheels make skateboards much safer than they used to be.

3

Avoid skateboards with wheels made of hard, skittery clay or rock-hard urethane. Watch out for ones with poor wheel clearance, too; the wheels will skid to a stop if they rub the board or the trucks as you turn, and you'll get dumped on the ground. If the hanger plates on an inexpensive board are real long, made of thin metal, and screwed in haphazardly, pass them by; they might break loose or bend.

The board itself should be made of good quality ply-wood or of solid hardwood with straight grain. If there's lots of grain run-out, as on the cheapo board shown, the board might break in half. If the top of the board is slick, you can buy it, but see page 40 for a method of putting non-slip grip tape on so your feet won't slide off.

There are many other ready-made boards, particularly ones made of polypropelene and pultruded fiberglass, that are quite a few notches above the super-cheapo model, and if you can get one of these with good equipment like the stuff described below, at a reasonable price, go ahead and get it; just make sure the equipment is serviceable, so you won't have to take it off the board, throw it away, and spend a whole lot more money replacing it.

If you have trouble finding a decent first board that's already put together, you can easily buy the parts and build up the board yourself. Not only will this often save you some money, it will also teach you about the skate-board as you go along, so you'll be able to take good care of it. Just pick a board top, trucks, and wheels, then get the tools you need and put it all together to make a first board that's just right for you.

PICKING A BOARD TOP

Before buying any board top, figure out what size is reasonable for you. There are endless sizes and shapes of skateboards for different tastes and different tricks, but to start out, you simply want to get a top that is big enough for you to stand on comfortably. To find out just how big that is, you have to measure the length of your normal stance. Get a yardstick, lay it on the floor, and stand on it as shown in Illustration 2. Notice that you need to have your feet spread just a little and turned *diagonally,* so the yardstick runs from the heel of your back foot to the toe of your front foot.

Which foot goes in front, you ask? The guy in Illustration 2 has his right foot forward. In most of the other illustrations and photos in this book, you'll notice that the riders have their left feet forward. Left foot forward is the most common stance, and the right-foot-forward stance is called "goofy-foot," but it makes no real difference. Put whichever foot forward that feels best. When you have gotten into a comfortable stance on the yardstick and have measured the heel-to-toe distance, add six inches to it, and you'll have the minimal length your first board can be. If, for instance, your stance length is 18 inches, you'll need a 24 inch board to start on, or one a little bigger. Lots of hot riders use smaller boards with great success, but for a start, it's nice to have plenty of foot-room. For this same reason, you should try to get a first board that is at least six inches wide at its widest part, and not too skinny back at the tail, something close to the general shapes given in Illustration 8.

illustration **2** Stance Measurement

When you have a size in mind for your first skateboard top, consider which sort of material you want the top to be made from. The number of possibilities is staggering. If you don't want to spend too much money on the board, you'll find that the field gets narrowed down right away.

If you have a little money saved up, on the other hand, you can start right out with a good fiberglass board. The trouble is, you have to pay out quite a bit to get a really good pultruded unidirectional glass board (one that is strong and light because of its pre-tensioned construction) or a carefully hand-laminated glass cloth board. These two good types can be made to have some flex and yet good memory and durability (see Illustrations 3, 4, 5). The expense is worth it in the long run, but for a newcomer to skateboarding, it may make sense to get a board out of some cheaper material.

Of the less expensive choices, three which make good sense are polypropelene, high-grade hardwood, and good old reliable plywood.

Polypropelene and other similar plastic mixtures or derived plastics like polyolefin and polyalymer are, for the most part, opaque (non-see-through), slightly rubbery, and very stable. They can be molded easily and cheaply into the shape of a skateboard top. The good things about board tops made from these plastics are many: they are usually very strong, they don't chip, splinter, or get sharp around the edges (which is nice when you're learning and falling down on them now and then), they usually have non-skid surfaces so you won't slip off them, and they don't wear out for a long time, unless you are very heavy and hard on them.

On the negative side, polypropelene type board tops have to be made thick in order to be strong enough, or they have to have thick ribs on their undersides. The thicker a skateboard is, the higher you rest above the wheels; the higher above the wheels you are, the more tippy the board is, especially when you try to turn it. Many people can get used to this tippiness and can learn to make it work for them, but as a beginner, it may throw you off for awhile. Polypropelene type boards also have the drawback of not being very resilient. If you are light (like under 95 pounds), you may find that the flex and the memory of some polypropelene type boards are pretty good for you; heavier riders may find similar plastic board tops saggy and very slow to remember how straight they were supposed to be (see Illustration 4). To match any prospective board top to *your needs,* there's a simple test you can make. Get a couple little blocks of wood that are about ¾" thick and two by six inches in size, or a little bigger. Take these Test Blocks with you whenever you go shopping for a skateboard top. If the prospective top has wheels attached, put it on the floor and place the blocks near the wheels, as in Illustration 3, to keep them from rolling. If the top you're looking at doesn't have wheels attached, just put the two Test Blocks down on the floor at about the distance apart that the trucks will be, and lay the top over the blocks. Then jump up and down on the top, like the guy in the illustration is doing. You'll be able to tell right away if the top is saggy (no memory) or too stiff (no flex), or just right. To me, "just right" means that the top flexes about ¾" (it will tap the floor if you have it on the Test Blocks) and then springs you back a little so you bounce up and down. I don't like board tops that flex way down like diving boards and then twang you up in the air and into a full gainer. Some people do, but then I think they should go into springboard diving instead of skateboarding.

For your beginning polypropelene type board, all you need is a little bit of flex without a lot of sag. Before you buy a polypropelene board top, check to see if it has guide holes drilled in the bottom of it for trucks. If it does, that's OK, but make sure you get trucks that match the holes, or you'll have to do some tricky redrilling.

One last warning about polypropelene type boards. A few have been made from very poor plastic that seemed OK when tested inside, but that got all saggy when warmed up out in the sun. If you are in doubt, ask around before buying a board that might turn into a noodle the first time you put it to good use.

"Blank" or unfinished tops for skateboards are also made from several hard and semi-hard woods, like ash, oak, birch, mahogany, and fir, among others. For strength, these are often made ¾" thick at least, unless they are very fancy and therefore out of the low price range. A cheap hardwood board will work OK if you make sure

illustration **3** No Flex

illustration **4** No Memory

illustration **5**
Flex and Memory

the grain is fairly tight and straight, with a minimum of "run-out" when you look at the board from the side. For a board with good grain, see Illustration 6; for one with too much run-out, look at Illustration 1. Thick wood boards, though a little tippy, will work fine for a beginner, and there are some old pros who swear by them for certain types of skateboarding, but they do not have any flex at all; also, they tend to crack and get splintery around the edges. Unless you put non-slip grip tape on them as in Illustration 26, many will also get slick and slippery after awhile. Super-good tops *can* be made from wood and from wood-plastic laminations, but only with a great deal of know-how and top grade hardwood. These types of boards will be discussed in the equipment sections of the special riding style chapters.

For those of you who just want to get a general idea of what skateboarding is about without spending hardly anything on a board top, there is good old plywood. One-half inch marine-grade mahogany plywood or even high grade douglas fir plywood of the same thickness will make a passable top for a first skateboard. Take a pattern from the samples provided in Illustration 8, fitting it to the length you got from measuring your stance and adding six inches. Or if you like the size and shape of a friend's board better, just turn it upside down and trace around it onto your plywood. Make sure you put the pattern on the plywood in such a way that the grain of the top ply is running lengthwise along the board, as in Illustration 7. This will give you the best strength you can get out of the plywood. Cut out the shape carefully with a sharp jig saw or coping saw or band saw or saber saw, whichever you can get ahold of. Rasp, file, and finally sand the edges of the board thoroughly, so they wind up as smooth and round as possible. One of the big problems with plywood boards is that they tend to get splintery around the edges when you bang them against sign-poles, curbs, kids' shins, and other hard things. One other drawback to plywood is that it has very little flex and memory, unless it is either very thin, which makes it too weak, or made up of fancy hardwoods that make it too expensive. But the regular ½" thick plywood will do in a pinch, and after all, a lot of us are in a pinch a lot of the time.

BUYING TRUCKS AND WHEELS

Now that you've picked the top for your first board, you need the rest of the outfit, the running gear that goes down underneath. At this point hitch in your belt and save a little dough. It isn't worth it to cut corners on the trucks and wheels, even for your first skateboard. The chintzy running gear is not only chintzy, but unsafe, noisy, and no fun. If, on the other hand, you make a good investment on running gear, you can change it quite

illustration **6** Tight, Straight Wood Grain

illustration **7**
Lengthwise Grain

illustration **8**
Two Board Top Patterns

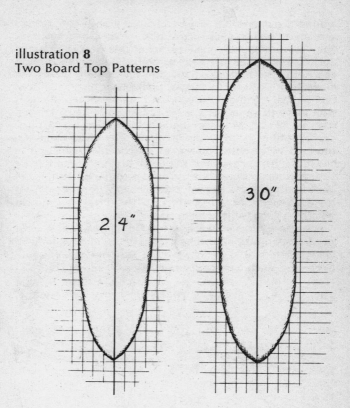

easily onto a more advanced top when you're ready to step up to a more advanced type of riding; this will save a lot of money for new equipment.

Among the many trucks (those are the metal gizmos, like the one in Illustration 9, that hold the wheels to the board top and allow you to turn by leaning) there are two old standbys and lots of good and bad newcomers.

Steel Chicago trucks have been doing good service on shoe skates for decades. They work very well on hardwood skating rinks, and are OK for most skateboards, too. The basic working parts are all strong and well-made, and Chicago trucks will last as long as most others in normal circumstances. They are cheaper and more readily available than many other trucks, too. One drawback they have, however, is a steel pivot that fits into a metal socket in the hanger plate without anything to cushion the joint. The metal-to-metal contact in there makes the ride precise at first, but after awhile the joint gets loose and rattly. Another problem with the Chicago truck is caused by its rigid strength. The flat mounting plate used on Chicago trucks is so rigid that if you put the truck on a flexible board, something has to give when the board tries to flex. Sometimes the board breaks; more often the hanger plate of the truck breaks. On most first boards, though, the Chicago truck (and the other all-steel trucks either designed like the Chicago type or made out of heavy-gauge stamped steel) will hold up fine and do what you need to have them do.

Sure Grip trucks like the one in Illustration 9 have been around for quite some time too, and they seem very well adapted to skateboarding, at least for those at the beginning and intermediate levels of ability. They are made from high-grade cast aluminum, except for the axles and the main bolts, which are hard steel. There is

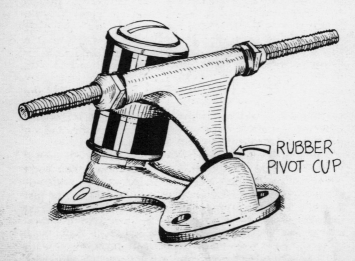

RUBBER PIVOT CUP

illustration 9 Sure Grip Double Action Truck

a rubber cup in the pivot socket of the Sure Grip truck, which makes for a quieter, smoother ride and cleaner turns than are possible with the all-steel trucks. The only weakness of the Sure Grip truck (and this goes for other aluminum trucks of similar design) is the soft aluminum of the threads in the hanger plate that the hard steel main bolt screws into (see Illustration 25). If you aren't careful, you can strip the soft hanger plate threads when you are trying to start screwing the main bolt into place, so BE CAREFUL when screwing the main bolt into an aluminum truck hanger plate. Sure Grip trucks have notoriously hard cushions that may give you trouble later on (see page 143), but they are plenty good for a start. Besides, Sure Grip trucks are much more durable than many steel-truck fans would like to admit; the soft aluminum hanger plate will not break, no matter how flexy a top you bolt it to. Under normal circumstances, and even under most slam-bang circumstances, the whole truck will hold up fine.

There are many, many other trucks beyond the two old stand-bys. Most of them are more expensive, and many of them are made mainly for special hot riding techniques. It doesn't make sense to spend all the money for these trucks if you aren't sure yet whether your future style will even call for them. Start with the basic trucks, and work up to the special equipment later. On the other hand, if you can't locate any Sure Grip or Chicago trucks, at least try to get decent trucks with rounded shapes as in Illustration 9, or ones with thick little buttresses for reinforcement, like those on the sturdy Super Surfer trucks. Cheaper trucks with thin metal parts and sharp inner corners are weak at the joints, especially where the yoke joins the truck body, and on the hanger plate as shown in Illustration 10.

You should get the best wheels you can afford, even if it seems like they cost more than they should. You don't have to buy super-wide-super-tall-double-shouldered-super-costly wheels, but you should try to get not just any old urethane wheels, but the wheels with the best urethane available, and with sealed precision bearings, if you can afford them. Good wheels will make your skateboard not only easier to ride and more fun to learn on, but also SAFER no matter what degree of expertise you develop up to.

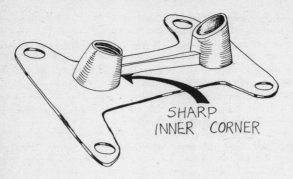

SHARP
INNER CORNER

illustration **10**

One type of sealed precision bearing wheel which is not too large or wide for a normal skateboard, and which is made out of really marvelous urethane is the "Road Rider Two." The wheel was thought up by a guy named Tony Roderick, who was lucky enough to have the help of a urethane company in the east that had long and valuable experience in making urethane wheels with good traction. This urethane company could control their urethane formulas so well that they were capable of making wheels for Xerox copiers that could whisk one piece of paper off the top of a stack without whisking off two. Next time you're around a copier, like the Xerox 3100 model, for instance, look into the machine where the pile of blank paper is. Lo and behold, back in there you can see a couple of urethane wheels that look an

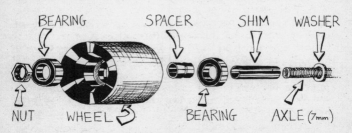

BEARING   SPACER   SHIM   WASHER

NUT   WHEEL   BEARING   AXLE (7mm)

illustration **11** Sealed Precision Bearing Wheel

awful lot like skateboard wheels. Heh. Anyway, Tony Roderick and some skateboard makers at N.H.S. Plastics in California worked out a sealed bearing wheel design, and told the great urethane company that they wanted a wheel made of urethane that would grip the road like a racing tire, last forever, and roll as fast as possible. The great urethane company went to work, and came up with something that was, at the time it first came out, *far* ahead of all other urethane wheels.

The only drawback to the Road Rider wheels is their cost. You can buy two cheap open-bearing wheels for the price of one Road Rider. But the Road Rider is still worth it, because it saves you many spin-outs, skids, wipe-outs, and broken bones. Also, you never have to waste time cleaning the bearings, and if you use them reasonably, the Road Rider wheels will last at least twice as long as most other wheels.

There are other slightly less expensive wheels that have been used with great success, such as the Stoker, made by Roller Sports, and the Power Paw, and the standard Metaflex wheel. All of these wheels have fair-to-good traction, and none of them spin out all of a sudden like the old clay wheels. But each type of wheel has some problem. The Stoker is so big and wide that it will tend to hit the bottom of your board (see page 153); the Power Paw is chattery and unpredictable in sharp turns on rough pavement, and the Metaflex wheels, though they last long, are a lot quicker to slide than the others. Besides, all of these older wheel types have open bearings, which are much more of a pain than the nice sealed ones.*

---

* A number of large wheels have appeared on the market, and a few extra wide ones as well. Although these special-size wheels are good for some special purposes, they often have drawbacks. The wide ones are slow unless they are made of hard urethane. The large diameter ones tend to have poor traction, and you often need to alter the board and add risers to get adequate clearance for sharp turns. Get the large or wide wheels only if you have a special need and are willing to do the alterations for them. One trick which improves the traction of the large wheels, especially those made of good urethane, is to ride them hard on a rough street surface; do controlled slides at low speed and you'll notice that little "ruffles" soon get built up on the surface of each wheel. These ruffles act like tire treads and make the wheels grip better.

Lately, many companies have been quick to imitate the design, the sealed bearings, the red color, and the high price of the Road Rider wheel. Some other wheels, like the super-expensive Bennett aligators, and the more reasonable orange OJ wheels, have chosen not to imitate, and have come up with different and improved shapes; but as far as I've seen, *nobody* has matched the magic urethane of the tried and proven Road Rider wheels. Chances are, they will some day soon. At last report, both Power Paws and Rolls Royce were making sealed bearing urethane wheels that were almost as good as, though somewhat different from the Road Riders. When skateboarders have tested and proven the new wheels with magic urethane, then you should try those wheels. But in the meantime save your money and try to get the proven Road Riders.

If there's just no way you can get the money together for top-grade sealed bearing wheels, you can use less expensive open bearing wheels. They'll work OK until you can step up to the sealed bearing ones made out of magic urethane. But BEWARE! Don't try to do fancy stunts on non-fancy wheels! You just can't pull off the same radical turns on regular wheels as the hot-shot riders can on their high-performance wheels. If you attempt such turns, you will find that at a certain critical point of strain, the regular urethane wheels will break loose, spin out, and put your body down on the asphalt. It's odd, isn't it, how pavement looks much smoother when seen from up above your board than when seen from very close, as you slide along on it. Get the idea? Even when you do get the good wheels, don't lose your head. They usually have a nice smooth way of easing into a slide when you push them hard, but they can be made to spin out too, if you get suicidal about it.

Two final words of warning when you're looking for your first wheels; don't get the ones with the rock-hard urethane cores, and don't get the ones with shielded "precision" self-contained bearings. You can pick out the wheels with the hard cores by first pushing your fingernail into the urethane at the edge of the rolling surface of the wheel that is closest to the truck, then pushing your fingernail into the inner edge of the wheel, by the

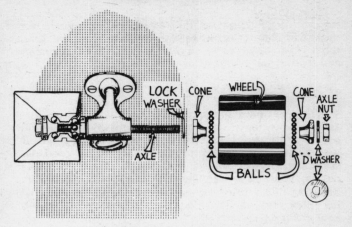

illustration **12** Open Bearing Wheels

bearing cup. If the inner edge is much harder, don't buy
the wheel. It will work OK at first, but as it wears down
it will get slicker and slicker as you get into harder and
harder urethane, until it has almost no traction at all. The
hard-core wheels are excellent for certain special types
of skateboarding, (see page 75 and page 113) but they're
not for beginners.

The self-contained or shielded "precision" bearings are
not dust-proof like the expensive sealed precision bearings, and when dirt gets into shielded bearing wheels,
you can't take them apart like you can take apart the
open bearing wheels. Moreover, these so-called "precision" bearings are often precise only when they're brand
new. After awhile they get loose and then you can't
adjust them to get rid of the looseness, and that's a real

illustration **13**
Shielded Bearing "Precision" Wheel

pain. So if you can't get the sealed bearing wheels like the Road Riders, or wheels that come close to Road Rider quality, get good adjustable open bearing wheels and learn how to adjust them as on page 36.

TOOLS

When you have settled on the trucks and wheels that are up to your quality standards, and low enough in price for you to afford, you have to get a couple tools for your running gear. First off, you'll need a good old skate key. Get one with a wrench end that fits the lock nut on your truck (see Illustration 25), and make sure it has a little screwdriver squashed out of the metal at the other end, one that fits into the screwdriver slot on your main bolt. Carry this key with you whenever you are skating, so you can keep the trucks adjusted and locked in place. Loose trucks can lead to dangerous "speed wobbles," and if the lock nut is left loose and the main bolt works its way out of its threads in the hanger plate, the result can be embarrassing (see Illustration 16).

If you are getting any kind of wheels other than the cheap ones made for roller skates, you'll need a double-ended socket tool to work on your wheels. There are two

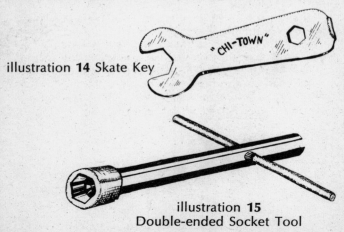

illustration **14** Skate Key

illustration **15**
Double-ended Socket Tool

illustration **16**

types, so make sure you get the tool with the sockets that fit the axle nuts and the cones (see Illustration 12) that came with your wheel. You don't have to carry this tool with you at all times, because the parts it fits don't need adjustment and rarely come loose, once they're set correctly.

There aren't many other tools needed for making a skateboard, other than a drill, a hammer, a screwdriver, a vise, and some other tools that you should be able to get ahold of easily.

HARDWARE

To round out the equipment necessary to get your first board put together, you'll need some little odds and ends of hardware, the sorts of things that make any project cost more than you counted on.

For instance, for each open bearing wheel (if you got that kind) you'll need two bearing cones, 16 3/16" ball bearings, a lock-washer (the thin black "vicious circle" kind), a "D" washer, and an axle nut. See Illustration 12 to get an idea of what all these parts are. For those of you who saved up and got Road Riders or some other sealed bearing wheels, all you need other than the parts that came with the wheel is the single axle nut and a small washer (see Illustration 11). If you are mounting a sealed bearing wheel on a large (5/16") axle you won't even need the adapting shim shown in the illustration. All wheel hardware, for either the open bearing or the sealed bearing wheels, should be available where you buy the wheel and the truck it is to go on; make sure, though, while you're still at the shop, that the stuff fits together; there are different sizes, and some parts are metric while others are Standard American size, which makes it tricky. At some good shops, you can get self-locking axle nuts, called "aero stop nuts." There is a little ring of nylon set right into each nut, so when you tighten it, it can't jiggle loose. These self-locking nuts don't cost much, and they save you a lot of worry, so get them if you can.

To hold the trucks to a polypropelene type board top, you need either 8-32 flat head phillips machine screws that are *just* long enough to go through your board,

the truck, and a nut, or number 8 hex-head sheet metal
screws that are long enough to go through the truck
hanger and well into the bottom of the board, but *not*
through the board. The sheet metal screws can only be
used on certain kinds of plastic boards; ask your dealer
if you aren't sure about yours. The sheet metal screws
will rattle loose if you use them on overly soft plastic
or on a wood board top. If you choose to use machine
screws on a polypropelene board, and want to keep
them from rattling loose, you can go to a big hardware
or building supply store and get self-locking "aero stop
nuts" to fit your 8-32 machine screws. They *never* come
off.

To hold your trucks to a hardwood or plywood board,
use 8-32 round head machine screws that are *just* long
enough to go through the board, the truck, and a nut.
If you don't want round screw-heads sticking up off the
top of your board, get 8-32 round head machine screws
that are somewhat shorter, namely, *not quite* long enough
to go through the trucks and the board; get number 8
Tee nuts too, and you'll be able to put them in flush
with the board's deck, as described on page 30.

If the deck of your chosen board top doesn't have a
non-skid textured deck, you can get neato non-slip grip
tape and put it on yourself. Go to a well-equipped skateboard outlet, or if you can't find one of those, a good
boat shop, and get a couple of feet of 1" tape, or 2"
tape if you want to be extravagant. It'll cost you a dollar
or two, but it'll save you from a lot of slip-slopping
around when you're trying to get your stance set up right
on the board, especially if you have a wood board; wood
gets slick after awhile. The non-slip tape has a rubbery
surface so you can even use it with bare feet if you want.

GETTING YOUR FIRST SKATEBOARD TOGETHER

All right. You have all the necessary parts and tools,
and you're ready to make your board now; let's get it
done quick so you can get into *riding* the thing. Each
kind of board requires a different hanger plate attachment procedure, so find the procedure that applies to
your board and go to it; when you get the hanger attached to your board top, go on to the wheel and truck

assembly sections, and the necessary adjustments, all of which are the same no matter what kind of top you have.

Hanger Plate Attachment on Polypropelene Type Board: First you have to take your trucks apart, so you can mount the hanger plates easily, without having to work around all the awkward machinery sticking up off them. Take out the handy skate key you got when you bought your trucks and loosen the lock nut on the main bolt (see Illustration 17), turning the nut counter-clockwise as you look at it from above the head of the main bolt. A half turn or so should do it. Hold the nut still with your fingers and use the screwdriver end of the skate key to unscrew the main bolt, counter-clockwise, all the way out. If the main bolt has a hex head, use a wrench to unscrew it. As it gets more and more unscrewed, the main bolt may get a little hard to turn because the cushions squish against it. Don't force things; you might strip the threads in the hanger plate, especially if it is an aluminum hanger plate. Loosen up the cushions by wiggling them around, then unscrew the bolt the rest of the way. When the end of the bolt comes out of the threads, twist the truck on its pivot so the main bolt points away from the threaded hole, then pull the truck up at an angle so the pivot comes out of its socket hole easily (see Illustration 17).

Now you can figure out where to put the hanger plate on the board top. Turn the top upside down and see if there are already little guide holes for the mounting screws that match the holes in your hanger plates. If there are matching guide holes, fine, you can skip the next four paragraphs and go on, but if there aren't any that match, you'll have to make your own.

To place the guide holes, first draw a center line with a flow pen from one end of the board to the other. If you can't tell where the line should go by using a line in the plastic or by running a yardstick from one pointed end of the board to the other, measure in equal distances from both sides at a couple places along the length of the board and make a center line that way (see Illustration 18). Once you have a good center line drawn, figure out how far apart the holes are on your hanger

illustration **17**
Pulling Truck Apart

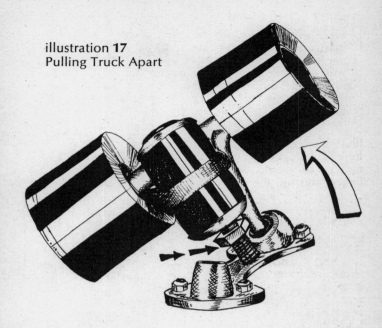

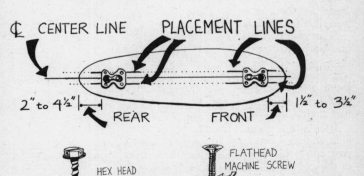

₵ CENTER LINE   PLACEMENT LINES

2" to 4½" | REAR   FRONT | 1½" to 3½"

HEX HEAD
SHEET METAL
SCREW

FLATHEAD
MACHINE SCREW

SELF-LOCKING
NUT

illustration **18** Placing Hanger Plates

plate (on a three-hole hanger plate, measure the distance between the two side-by-side holes); divide the distance in half, measure out that much on either side of your center line, and draw placement lines as in Illustration 18. If you are setting the board up for Sure Grip trucks, you'll find that the holes are about an inch apart; measure out ½″ from the center line on either side, and you can make placement lines that may be seen through the holes in the hanger plates. Once you have all of the placement lines drawn, you can put the hanger plates anywhere you want along them; for general, all-around use, however, it's best to start with the outer end of each plate about two and half to three inches in from the closest end of the board. When you have the hanger plates where you want them, make sure they are both set with the PIVOT ENDS OUTWARD (toward the ends of the board) and the MAIN BOLT ENDS INWARD (toward the center of the board). That means that on each hanger, the big threaded hole has to be closest to the center of the board, and the pivot socket has to be toward the end of the board. If you are mounting hanger plates with a three-hole pattern, like the Chicago ones, just make sure the hole that isn't lined up on the placement lines is *exactly* lined up on the center line of the board.

Leave the hanger plates in place while you do the following drilling procedure, so the holes in the board will be sure to come out matching the holes in the hanger plates. If you plan to use sheet metal screws, drill with a 3/32″ bit, and make sure your guide holes are in the middle of the hanger plate holes. For machine screws, use a 5/32″ drill bit to make the guide holes. Whichever bit you use, try hard to hold the hanger plate completely still and drill *straight down* into the board, so the fasteners will stay lined up when you tighten them. On hanger plates like the Sure Grip one, which have oval-shaped screw holes placed very near to the big metal bulges for the pivot and main bolt holes, drill the guide holes toward the *outside* of the oval hole (see Illustration 19). That'll make it easy to get the fastener in without getting it hung-up against the nearby metal bulge.

The small guide holes for the sheet metal screws only need to go in about ½″. If you don't think you can keep the drill from zipping all the way down through the soft

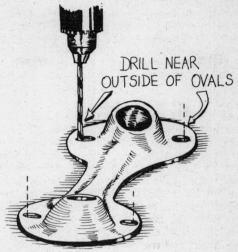

illustration 19
Drilling Guide Holes

polypropelene, wrap tape around the drill bit ½″ up from the end (similar to what is shown in Illustration 21), and it'll keep the drill from going in any farther.

For those of you drilling the wider (5/32″) guide holes for flat head machine screws, after you have drilled each hole, run the drill in and out of the hole a bunch of times, then push a machine screw into it; this will make it easier to keep the hanger plate still while you drill the other holes. When you finish drilling all the holes, take the machine screws out, turn the board over, and do the counter-sinking with a counter-sinking drill bit. Be careful not to make the counter-sinking too deep, or it will weaken the board. Push the machine screws down through the board and the hanger plates. Start your self-locking (aero stop) nuts onto the machine screw threads (clockwise), and turn them by hand until it gets hard to. Now you're set to do the Big Cinch-down.

Tightening the flat head machine screws into the self-locking nuts is a real chore. Make sure the screws aren't any longer than they need to be. If they're much too long, you'll just have to do that much extra sweating and blistering-the-hands to get them tight, and you may have to cut the ends of the screws off anyway if they stick up where the wheels might hit them. When you have the machine screws in place and the self-locking nuts started onto their threads, put the whole skateboard into a vise with the phillips heads of the machine screws facing toward you, and the grip of the vise jaws near the hanger plate (see Illustration 20). Then take an open-end or adjustable (crescent-type) wrench and get it set on one of the nuts behind the board; get a phillips screwdriver that fits snugly and put it into the corresponding screw, push the screw all the way into its counter-sunk hole, and start to work. It'll take some time. And some sweat and cussing maybe. But work slowly and keep pushing hard on the screwdriver whenever you're trying to turn it so you don't strip the x-shaped slots out of the head of the machine screw. When you get each machine screw and nut almost tight, leave it and get the others down to that almost-tight point, then you can do the

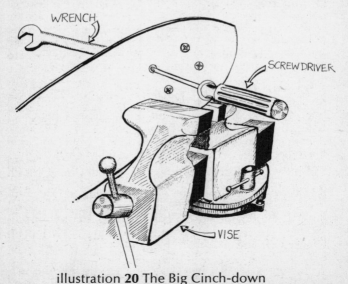

illustration **20** The Big Cinch-down

last hard turn by holding the screwdriver still and turning each nut with the wrench for extra leverage. Just don't get carried away and strip the threads on the nut, now that you've done all the work to get it where you want it. When the nuts are all tight, go on to *"Wheel and Truck Assembly,"* page 32.

If you have sheet metal screws and tiny little guide holes, the best way to start the screws in is with a nut driver, which is just like a screwdriver, except the end of it is made so it can help you drive the hex-head screw in without being driven nutty, or screwy, or whatever. If you can't get a nut driver, look and see if there is a screwdriver slot for starting the sheet metal screw, like there is on the sheet metal screw in Illustration 18. If you have neither a nut driver, nor a screwdriver slot to help you start the sheet metal screws, just use an adjustable (crescent-type) wrench, adjusting it carefully to the size of the hex head of the screw; hold the wrench up vertically, so it's easier to press down and start the screw straight in the guide holes. When the screws have been turned clockwise into the board about a quarter inch or so, you can use the adjustable wrench in the normal out-to-the-side way. It will soon get so hard to turn the screw that you'll have to use the wrench that way to get the screw in at all. Just take your time and keep the wrench adjusted carefully so it doesn't slip and round off the hex shape of the screw head. If you're using the nut driver, you may find that it won't fit between the hex head of the screw and the metal bulge of the hanger plate. Resort to an adjustable wrench and keep at it until you have all of the screws in very tight, then go on to *"Wheel and Truck Assembly,"* page 32.

Hanger Plate Attachment on a Wood Board: Hardwood and plywood boards of the basic beginner's quality both require the same assembly procedure. Take your trucks apart before you start the hanger attachment procedure, so you can mount the hanger plates without having to work around all the awkward truck machinery sticking up off them. Take out the handy skate key you bought with your trucks and loosen the lock nut on the main bolt (see Illustration 18), turning the nut counterclockwise as you look at it from above the head of the main bolt. A half turn or so will loosen it enough. Then turn the key around and use the screwdriver end to unscrew the main bolt, counter-clockwise, holding the lock nut still with your fingers at the same time. A few main bolts have hex heads; for these you use the wrench. As the main bolt turns farther and farther up, it may get a little hard to turn because the cushions squish against it (see Illustration 25). Loosen things up by wiggling the cushions around. When the bolt is all the way unscrewed, don't try to yank the truck straight up out of the holes in the hanger plate; twist it on the pivot so the main bolt points away from the threaded hole, then pull the truck up at an angle so the pivot comes out of its hole easily. That way you'll be sure not to mess up those delicate threads in the main bolt hole, especially if the hanger plate is made of soft aluminum.

Now you can figure out where to put the hanger plate on the bottom of the board. Assuming that there are no guide holes on the board, your first chore will be making placement lines so you can drill your own holes for the hanger plates.

First draw a light pencil line down the center of the board from one end to the other. If the board is like the ones shown in Illustration 8, this will be easy; you can just draw the center line from one pointed tip to the other. But if you have a round-ended or square-ended board (square corners really should be rounded off to avoid splinters and cuts), measure in equal distances from both sides of the board at a couple of points along its length and make a center line like the one in Illustration 18. Once you have your center line drawn, figure out how far apart the holes are on your hanger plate (on a three-hole plate like the Chicago one, measure the distance between the two side-by-side holes), divide that distance in half, and measure that much out to each side from the center line so you can draw placement lines like those in Illustration 18. If you are setting the board up for Sure Grip trucks, you'll find that the holes are an inch apart (two of the holes are a little farther apart than that, but the one inch measurement will do just to get the placement lines). Measure out one-half inch on both sides of the center line to get your placement lines. Once you have the lines drawn, you can put the hanger plates

anywhere you want to along them; for all-around use,
however, it's best to have the outer end of each plate
about two and a half to three inches in from the end of
the board. When you have them where you want them,
make sure both hanger plates are set with the PIVOT
ENDS OUTWARD (toward the ends of the board) and the
MAIN BOLT ENDS INWARD (toward the center of the
board). That means that on each hanger plate the big
threaded hole has to be closest to the center of the
board; the other hole, which usually has a little rubber
cup in it, goes closest to the end of the board. If you
aren't SURE you have the hangers right, look at Illustration 18; you can see the black rubber cups at the pivot
ends. Got it now? Good, because if you do it backwards, the board won't steer the way you aim it. If you
are mounting a hanger plate with a three-hole pattern,
like the Chicago one, make sure the hole that doesn't
line up on the placement line *does* line up *exactly* on the
center line.

During the following guide-hole drilling procedure,
leave the hanger plate in place so the holes in the board
will be sure to come out matching the holes in the
hanger plate. Put a 5/32" bit in your drill, hold the hanger
plate still, and drill the holes *straight* down through the
board, so the machine screws will stay lined up when you
tighten them. On hanger plates like the Sure Grip ones
that have oval screw holes placed very near to the metal
bulges for the pivot and main bolt holes, drill the guide
holes for the machine screws toward the *outside* of each
oval hole (see Illustration 19). As you finish drilling each
hole, run the bit in and out a bunch of times, then push
a machine screw into the hole. This will make it easier
for you to hold the plate still as you drill the remaining
holes. Does this seem like a lot of fuss? It is, but the point
is that unless you do this job JUST RIGHT, the board
won't hold together and steer straight.

When all the holes are drilled, you have to do one of
two different procedures to get the machine screws
cinched down, depending on which length you got in the
hardware section above (page 20). If you got the longer
machine screws, the ones that will wind up with their
heads sticking up on the board deck, do the cinch-down
procedure described immediately below. If you got the

shorter machine screws and the Tee nuts that'll wind up flush with the board deck, skip two paragraphs down and do your cinch-down as described there.

To prepare for the *long-machine-screw cinch-down,* take the machine screws out of the holes first, then turn the board over and push them through from that side. Start the self-locking nuts on (clockwise) by hand until they get hard to turn.

Tightening the machine screws into the self-locking nuts takes a lot of leverage and sweat. To make the job as easy as possible, first make sure the machine screws aren't any longer than they need to be to get through the board, the hanger plate, and the nut. If they're too long, you'll just have to do that much more straining and twisting to get them tightened down, and you may have to cut the extra end off the screw anyway if it sticks up where the wheel will hit it. When you have the nuts hand-screwed onto your correct-length machine screws, put the whole skateboard into a vise with the machine screw heads toward you and the vise jaws gripping near the hanger plate (see Illustration 20). Then hold the nut still with an open-end or adjustable (crescent-type) wrench in one hand, and with the other hand grab a screwdriver that fits the screw snugly. Push each screw head all the way into its hole so it'll stay put against the deck when you start twisting it. The twisting takes some time, and maybe even a little cussing, but work slowly and remember to keep pushing hard on the screwdriver whenever you're trying to turn it, so you don't strip the slots out of the heads of the machine screws. When each screw and nut are almost tight, leave them and turn the others all to that almost-tight point. Then you may be able to do the last turn or so by holding the screwdriver in place on each screw and turning the nut with the wrench for extra leverage. On Sure Grip trucks the close proximity of the big bulge may keep the nut from turning. If you can use a wrench for the last hard turn, just don't use so much oomph that you strip the threads on the nut and wreck it after all the trouble you've gone to.

The cinch-down of the *short machine screw and Tee nut* requires more preparation but less muscle-work than the long screw method. To start with, you have to make sure you have EXACTLY the right length machine screw.

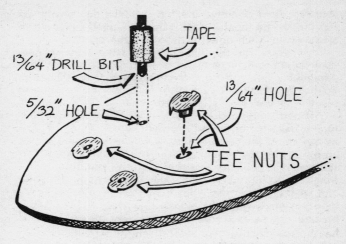

illustration **21** Tee Nut Assembly

The screw must be just a teeny bit less than long enough to go through the hanger plate and the board. Try one out, pushing it through from the hanger plate side. You may need a washer to make the length right. If your board is ¾" thick, a 1" machine screw with a washer will be about the right length. If the board is made from ½" plywood, a ¾" screw with a washer should work. Make sure the screw winds up almost long enough to reach through the board, though, or the Tee nut won't hold.

OK, when you have the right length machine screw, you have to widen out the guide holes so you can put the Tee nuts in place on the board's deck. Use a 7/32" drill bit to do the widening, and do it very carefully to make sure you don't make a wide hole right through the board. You only need a wide hole that goes in ¼". It's hard to drill that deep by guess-work; wrap some tape around the drill bit ¼" up from the tip, as shown in Illustration 21, and you'll be able to drill all the holes to the right depth in a jiffy. When the holes are widened out on the deck side of the board, put the top down on a flat surface and hammer the Tee nuts in until they are flush against the deck. If you plan to skate barefoot, you can take the extra precaution of filing around the edge of each Tee nut before you hammer it in, just to make sure there are no corners sticking up to scratch your feet on.

Once you have all the Tee nuts hammered in, put washers on the machine screws if you need to, then place the hanger plates (remember, PIVOT ENDS OUTWARD, MAIN BOLT ENDS INWARD) and you're almost ready to screw the machine screws in. Stop a moment though, before you cinch things down. Check one screw to see if it's going to be the right length. Then, if you want to be sure that the screws will never come loose, go buy or borrow some Loctite thread sealing resin. The strongest kind of Loctite is the "stud 'n' bearing mount," which is a cherry red fluid that will seal any threaded part so thoroughly that you may never be able to get it loose, even if you want to. Locktite "lock 'n' seal" is a blue thread sealing resin with medium strength, which means that it will stay right in most conditions, but you can loosen it with normal tools. "Lock-it" is another brand name for a blue resin like the Locktite "lock 'n' seal," and it works about the same. All of these thread sealers are pretty expensive, and you don't need very much of them, so instead of buying a whole tube's worth, try to borrow a tube and use a couple drops, if you can find a friend or parent who is an automotive machinist or mechanic. All you have to do to use the thread sealer is to put a drop or two on the end of the threads of each machine screw, then tighten it thoroughly. If you let the assembled unit sit for a couple hours, the sealer will harden in the threads and the machine screw will NEVER come loose.

After the machine screws are thoroughly tightened and sealed into place, you can check the Tee nuts and the ends of the machine screws to see if any sharp little edges are sticking up on the deck of the board. A fine metal file and some rough emery paper will round off these edges quickly, and your board will be ready for its Wheels and Trucks.

Wheel and Truck Assembly

No matter what kind of board you have put together, you will need to follow the steps below for putting your

wheels onto your trucks and attaching your trucks to the
hanger plates that you now have firmly anchored to your
board top.

To start the wheel assembly, first unscrew (counter-
clockwise) the lock nut that's on the end of the main
bolt, and take off the metal cushion caps and the cushions so the truck and the main bolt parts are separate.
Now you can work on the truck easily. The next steps
are different, depending on whether you have sealed
precision bearing wheels like the Road Riders (Illustration 11), or open bearing wheels (Illustration 12).

Before starting *Sealed Bearing Assembly,* you'll probably have to take off the two cones that the manufacturers put on your trucks. Those cones are for open
bearings, not for you. Unscrew (counter-clockwise) each
cone all the way off the axle, but leave the lockwashers
that are under them, (a small washer as in Illustration 11
is best, but a lockwasher will suffice). Sometimes the
cones have been put on with a powerful air-wrench, so
you have to put the truck in a vise (as in Illustration 23)
and get a box-end or carefully adjusted adjustable wrench
with a lot of leverage to undo the cone. Just make sure
you are loosening each cone counter-clockwise as you
look at it from the end of the axle. Start putting the
wheel parts on by slipping the adapting shim, the inside
bearing, and the spacer together. Push all three onto the
axle at once (see illustration 22). If you happen to have a
big 5/16″ thick axle, instead of the smaller and more

illustration **22** Assembling Sealed Bearing Wheel

common 7 millimeter size, you don't need the shim; just slide the inside bearing and the spacer right onto the axle. If the bearings you got are the handy single-seal type, make sure you get the sealed side toward the truck so it will keep dirt and water out of the bearings. If you have the bearings with seals on both sides, they aren't as easy to lubricate (see page 141), but they are easier to assemble because you don't have to worry about which side is in and which is out. When you have the inside bearing and the spacer in place, push the wheel over the inside bearing, then push the outer bearing into place, making sure the sealed side is out if it's the single-seal type. If you have put both single seal bearings on correctly, you won't be able to see the ball bearings now. Use the non-business end of a clothes pin to shove the bearing in if it's too hard to do with your fingers. Screw the axle nut on (clockwise) until it is finger tight, but DO NOT TIGHTEN IT!!! Tightening the axle nut on one end of the axle without putting anything on the other end will just pull the axle out of the truck. Assemble the second wheel the same way you did the first, and if you tightened the first axle nut a little by mistake and pulled the axle out a bit (I know, you were too excited about your hot new wheels and didn't notice the warning) all you have to do is loosen (counter-clockwise) the axle nut that you tightened too much, then tighten (clockwise) the axle nut on the other end of the axle to even things up. It may take a little jockeying back and forth, but get it so you have equal amounts of axle sticking out of the two axle nuts. Then tighten both nuts firmly, each a little at a time. Careful; it's easy to strip the threads on many axles because they are made of soft steel. If you do strip an axle see *Axle Threads Stripped,* page 152, for the remedy. When you have the two wheels on, assemble the two on the other truck, then skip down to the paragraphs on the final assembly and adjustment of the truck. You're almost done!

To *Assemble Open Bearing Wheels,* start by putting a truck into a vise as shown in Illustration 23. Be careful not to mash the curved part of the yoke; just stick the flat end of it into the vise jaws. Tighten the inside cones (clockwise) firmly so they'll stay put for good. Then take a wheel in hand and hold it with the *inner* side (this will be the side with the metal bearing cup near to the flat side surface of the wheel, and it'll also be the side without writing on it) facing up toward you, as shown. Turn the outer cone onto the axle (clockwise) a few turns, so the wheel can't fall off, then dribble the first eight ball bearings down into the race. Some people find it easiest to feed them in from between their fingers, as shown; others like pinching up one ball bearing at a time to make sure none get lost; do whatever seems to work best for you. If you don't have a vise, do this job over a spread-out rag to catch any loose ball bearings.

It seems to me that no matter what way *I* try to get those squirrely little devils in there, one or two always pop out of the wheel, take a bounce on the table, then roll off across the floor at top speed in search of some inaccessible corner where they can hide from me. Bah! If you get to hate fiddling with loose ball bearings and

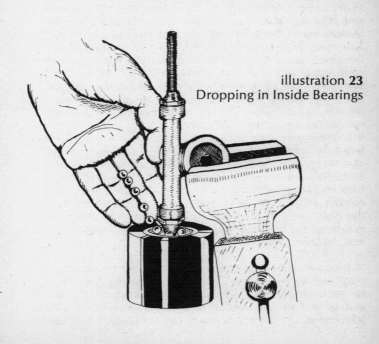

illustration **23**
Dropping in Inside Bearings

searching all over for them when they run away, save your money so you can get sealed bearing wheels. Those sealed bearings are much harder to lose. Roller skate bearings can be bought in metal retainer rings, and they're much cheaper than the sealed bearings, as are the wheels with shielded bearings, but both these convenience-oriented wheels are really a big pain. You can't clean either type, the shielded kind can't be adjusted, and the retainer type tend to self-destruct. So the choice is either to fool with the open bearings, or to save the pile of dough for the sealed bearing wheels.

When you get the first eight balls into your open bearing wheel by hook or by crook, press the wheel up against the bearings and turn it with your hand to get the balls lined up in the race, then hold the wheel in place against the bearings, loosen the vise, turn the truck over so the half-filled wheel is on top as in Illustration 24, then tighten the vise again (careful with that yoke) and put the other eight ball bearings into the outside race. Quickly now, before those treacherous little balls can organize a break-out, screw the outer cone in (clockwise) until it snugs down on the bearings. You may have to wiggle the wheel a little or even take the truck out of the vise and turn it over once more to get the balls into their races, but when they've finally gotten in line, screw the cone on hand tight so they can't get away. After the cone comes the "D" washer, then the axle nut to hold the whole works in place.

Bearing Adjustment: There is a neat way to adjust the bearings if you have one of those double-ended socket tools to fit your axle nuts and cones; tighten the cone (clockwise) onto the bearings until the wheel is just a little hard to turn, then tighten the axle nut in with your fingers as far as you can. Finally, put the socket tool onto the cone again, and turn the cone *counter-clockwise,* so it loosens itself off the bearings, but tightens against the "D" washer and axle nut. On almost all wheels this method will put the bearings in perfect adjustment; the wheels will spin freely and with just a tiny bit of looseness, but they won't be too loose; you want that tiny bit of looseness because when the wheels heat up while in use the urethane expands; if there is no slack, the bearings will get tight and overload, so they will wear out

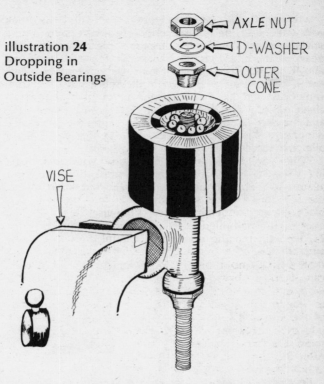

illustration **24**
Dropping in
Outside Bearings

AXLE NUT

D-WASHER

OUTER CONE

VISE

fast or even seize up. Check the wheel by spinning it and trying to wiggle it. There should be a bit of loose-ness. Readjust the bearings if they are too tight or so sloppy that the wheel can wobble all over the place; just loosen (counter-clockwise) the axle nut and start the adjustment procedure over again. Load the bearings in the other wheels, using the same method you used on the first one, and making sure you get eight balls in each race, sixteen balls in each wheel. Adjust all the wheels, and you're ready to put your board together and get it *on!* One little warning though before we leave the open bearings: DON'T OIL THEM!!! Skateboard bearings work best dry. Oil makes them get dirty so they go slow, rather than fast.

Mounting and Adjusting Trucks: To mount the truck and wheel units on the hanger plates, first reassemble the cushion caps, the rubber cushions, the main bolt, the yoke of the truck and the lock nut for each truck, as shown in Illustration 25. Just spin the lock nut on a few turns (clockwise) so the whole assembly stays together, but loose and flexible. Push the pivot of the truck all the way into the rubber cup in its socket (or into the bare socket, if there is no rubber cup), then carefully align the main bolt so it will screw at that slight angle into the threaded hole in the hanger plate. Eyeball the bolt and the hanger from different sides to make sure

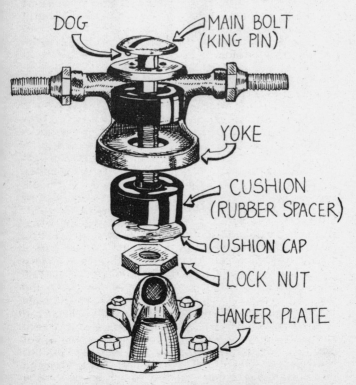

DOG

MAIN BOLT
(KING PIN)

YOKE

CUSHION
(RUBBER SPACER)

CUSHION CAP

LOCK NUT

HANGER PLATE

illustration **25** Truck Assembly

you have things lined up before you start twisting the bolt in at the wrong angle and stripping the threads out. It's especially easy to strip the threads in aluminum hanger plates like the Sure Grip ones, so if you have that type, WATCH THEM THREADS!! Start screwing the bolt in (clockwise) slowly, and stop if there is any resistance. You may have to wiggle and tug the cushions around to make sure the bolt has enough free play to get lined up with the threaded hole. Take your time. Get that bolt started right. Once you're sure the main bolt is started correctly in its threads, hold the nut still with your fingers and screw the bolt in (clockwise) with the screwdriver end of the skate key until it gets snug against the cushions. Now spin the nut down (clockwise) until it is just about to go tight against the hanger plate. Hold it still again and turn the main bolt in farther. Make sure the cushions and cushion caps are all meshed together so you can snug the bolt right down on them.

When the bolt is tight enough that the wheels can only pivot back and forth a quarter inch or so, turn the nut clockwise the last bit with the skate key until it is locked against the hanger plate good and tight. Now check the wheels again, trying to rock them on the trucks with your hands. They should have no more than a quarter inch of free movement. This setting is *much* too tight for normal skateboarding, but it is good for a beginner, because as a beginner, you will have plenty of trouble keeping the board from shooting out either in front of you or behind you; you won't want to worry about it wobbling loosely from side to side as well. Later on, as you learn to balance, you will want to loosen the truck bolts a good deal so you can turn more easily. Just remember, though, right from the start, that whenever you change the adjustment of the main bolt, you must LOCK THE NUT AGAINST THE HANGER PLATE!! Otherwise, the bolt will either strip out or come loose and suddenly allow the wheels to depart from the board, which can be an unpleasant surprise (see Illustration 16). Make a final check of your running gear to make sure you've got the trucks going the right direction. Are the cushions and the heads of the main bolts of both trucks closer to the center of the board than the wheel axles? Look at Illustration 6 for comparison. See how the cushions are toward the center of the board, and how the pivots point out toward the ends of the board? What's that? You just realized that you mounted one of the truck hangers backwards? Ack! Oh well, it just proves good old Murphy's law; "If a thing can be done wrong, it *will* be done wrong." If you got one of the trucks backwards, first remove it, then switch the hanger around so you have the PIVOT END OUTWARD and drill new guide holes if necessary, then come back for the Finishing Touches described just below.

Finishing Touches: There are a few last little things you can do to your new skateboard to make it just that much nicer than the other ones on the block; see if you can pick up the following handy items from your friendly local skateboard dealer.

For wood and smooth plastic tops, there's non-slip grip tape, which was already mentioned under the hardware paragraph. It is also known as foot-tred, or non-skid deck tape (that's what they call it in boat stores). It is wonderful stuff. If you have trouble finding it, you can get a lower quality tape from a building supply store that will do in a pinch, it's a non-skid tape used on tile floor and bathtubs. It works OK, but doesn't have quite the gripping power of the real bumpy non-slip tape made for skateboards and boats. All you need to do is cut a few strips of the tape and round off the corners with a pair of scissors, then take the paper off the back and stick the strips to your board as shown in Illustration 26. Your feet will never slip off the board again. And the stuff is rubbery, so it even feels OK under bare feet.

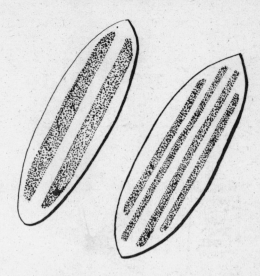

illustration **26** Non-slip Grip Tape

For those of you using open bearings, there is a dry lubricant that you can spray into the wheels for a super-quiet super low-friction roll that almost matches that of the sealed bearings. It is called Super Skate Spray, and it is a light, fast-evaporating liquid that dries up and leaves millions of tiny round particles of this white stuff behind. Those little white balls do wonders. They surround your bearings like millions of microscopic ball bearings, so everything just rolls and flows without any opposition. A less elegant type of dry lubricant, one which uses the slippery quality of graphite, is available under the names dri-slide and dry-lube; you might be able to find it at a good automotive service supply, if you don't have a local skateboard store that carries Skate Spray. Do not use *any* liquid lubricant like oil or grease for your skateboard wheels; liquid lubricants work OK for about a half minute, then they attract dirt and grit, and pretty soon the bearings wear down.

2

Your First Ride

You have now bought or made a good skateboard that fits you, and you have adjusted the trucks so that they can hardly turn at all (see page 38) if you haven't done this tight adjustment). You are ready for the first big step. Almost. Put on some heavy clothes and a pair of garden gloves and a pair of elbow pads to soften any fall which, by some strange fluke, you may happen to take even though you are following the almost foolproof learning method described below. Do not wear heavy shoes, though. The closer your feet are to being in contact with the surface of the skateboard, the better your control will be. In fact, if you have tough feet (like if you go around barefoot a lot) you can do your first low-speed learning without any shoes at all. Skateboarding at higher speeds without shoes is a risky proposition, but it's OK to do your first slow attempts barefoot. If you have tender feet, wear thin-soled tennis or running shoes so you get the feel of balancing a skateboard as quickly as possible, without having to learn through the interference of an inch or so of crepe or leather.

The basic idea of learning to do anything on a skateboard is to work up to it slowly. If you try to get ahead of yourself at any point, you take the risk of coming down hard and unexpectedly on that unforgiving pavement. So maybe start by standing on the board with it resting on something that keeps it from moving at all, like a scrap of old carpet, or a soft lawn, either of which will keep the wheels from rolling. That's a pretty slow

illustration **27**   . . . **28** "Goofy Foot"
Standard Stance   Stance

start, isn't it? But there's a point to it. If you stand on the
board when it can't roll, your feet can get the feel of the
size and shape of the board, and you can learn what
happens when you shift your weight around on it. Stand
with your feet at a forty-five degree angle across the
board, and with one in front of the other, whichever one
feels right (see Illustration 27, 28). With your feet in the
diagonal stance, tip the board from side to side. It can
get precarious, can't it? Bend your knees a little, and
it'll be easier to tip the board without falling off. Bend
over and look at the wheels as you tip the board. See how
they steer? Ahh. So works a skateboard. The wheels are
adjusted so tight at this point that you won't be able to
pivot them around too much, but you'll still be able to
get the idea. You tip to the right, the wheels steer to the
right. Not just the front wheels, but the rear ones as
well. It's an elegant little system, like a car with four-

wheel steering. Only better because it doesn't use up
any unreplenishable resources, like gas, oil, and at-
mosphere. You won't appreciate the full elegance,
though, until you start moving, I mean MOOOOOOV-
ING on the skateboard; flowing, pumping, wedeling,
power sliding. So let's get out to the pavement.

Find someplace where there is a smooth, gradual incline that levels out after going downhill for a few yards.
A place with relatively soft landing areas all around it is
best, like a driveway with lawns on both sides, or a
deserted walkway in a park. Check around on the pavement and make sure it is free of all pebbles that are
larger than pea-size. Why worry about little pebbles?
Because they can stop the wheels (especially if they are
hard wheels), and send you flying onto your face. So
when you've cleared the pebbles away, start at the top of
your clean little slope, standing next to the board with
one foot on it (see Illustration 29). I always like starting
with my front foot on the board; that way you push
off conveniently with your back foot and just slip it onto
the back of the board. There are many riders who start
with the back foot on the board, but unless you feel that
it's much easier to do it this way, try starting with your
front foot on the board. For your first attempt, you may
want a big strong friend to stand by and let you reach
one hand out and hold his shoulder just to get you going.
To keep from getting into the habit of leaning on the
friend (friends get tired of that sort of thing) let go as
soon as you are rolling. To get rolling, start off by giving
a little push with the foot that's on the ground. You don't
have to put your pushing-foot on the board right away
—it's kind of nice to keep it close to the ground, so in
case you lose your balance or the board starts to squirt
out in front of you or behind you, you can just set that
pushing-foot down and avoid a fall. But once you begin
to coast any distance at all, put the pushing-foot up on
the board and just cruise on down the gentle incline.
Wheeee!

Well, maybe only half a whee at that speed, and a lot
of wobbles. But that's OK; your speed will build up and
your ankles will get stronger and less wobbly in due time.
Just concentrate on keeping your knees bent a little,
and try to look forward, instead of down at the board,

illustration **29** Starting Stance **30** Coasting Downhill

so your feet will learn by themselves the feel of the
board's deck, and the rest of you will get into going
straight along without wobbling around too much. Some
people find that they are steadier if they put their hands
out in front of their bodies a little. Don't flap your elbows
all over the place, just move your hands forward from
your waist, as in Illustration 30. It makes you look like
you know what you're doing, even if it doesn't help your
balance much. When you can coast down your little
incline with grace, dignity, and no more than one
skinned limb for every three runs, add a little pushing
to your repertoire. As you slow down at the bottom of
the incline, carefully remove your pushing-foot from the
board and try a dab or two at the pavement to extend
your ride; you can use either foot (see Illustrations 31,
32), but I think the back foot is safest. Next time down,
dab a little harder, and, for a couple more rides, keep
adding to the effort until you can really propel yourself
at a decent fast-walk type clip. Say, you know, you're
looking pretty good. You can try to walk up to the nose
of the board and hang ten, and practice a whoop-tee-
doodle or two at this point if you want, then go on to
turning. There's a whole new concrete world about to
open to you!

Turning has to be learned by stages. There doesn't
seem to be any limit to the sharp turns hot-shots can do

illustration **31** Front Foot Pushing Along

illustration **32** Back Foot Pushing Along

on modern skateboards, but you have to learn to control the turns a bit at a time, starting with very slow, wide-radius ones, then shortening and shortening the radius and increasing the speed as you get more and more proficient. Do your first turns coasting slowly down your clean, gently sloping incline; tip the board very slightly with your feet, just thinking "turn, feet" instead of suddenly flexing your foot muscles and making the board dart to one side. When you can do a nice gentle arc of a turn at slow speed, try a push or two at the top of the incline so you can do the same wide arc with a little speed. Right away you'll notice that Isaac Newton's laws about bodies in motion come into play. They will work very noticeably on *your* body as you try to turn at speed. You must lean into any turn to keep from falling off the board and continuing to travel in a straight line until you are stopped by opposing forces, namely gravity and friction against the ground. The most effective way to counter the Newtonian problem when turning is to lean *before* the board is all the way into the turn, and to lean forward a little, as well as to the side, so that the board will, in effect, come up under you as it corners, instead of squirting out ahead as it tries to escape the added weight you put on it with centrifugal force. As you lean forward and into a turn, though, do not "broad-cast" the turn by twisting your head, shoulders and hips before the board starts to come around. This not only looks silly (as if you want everybody to know just how dramatic a turn you are about to make), it also torques your body out of alignment and balance over the board, and sets you up for an according-to-Newton fall.

illustration **33** Hanging Ten

illustration **34** Whoop-tee-doodle

Geez, all that sounds complicated. You don't have to understand the physics, though. Just lean forward and into your turns without twisting your body (as in Illus-trations 35 and 36), and you'll *feel* that neato dip and swoop that means you have Newton beat all to hell. Be sure to recover fully at the end of each swooping turn before you try another one, though; the ends of turns are precarious because when all the centrifugal force goes away, there isn't much left keeping you steady on the board; until your ankles are stronger, you will tend to wobble after going through a sharp turn.

After you have done only a few learning turns you will notice that you can already tip the board hard enough to make it tilt up on the edges of the wheels; this uncontrollable tilting is due to the fact that the trucks are tightened too much. It's time to loosen the

illustration **35** Right Turn   illustration **36** Left Turn

main bolts. Take out your trusty skate key, loosen
(counter-clockwise) each lock nut about a half turn or
so, then loosen (counter-clockwise) each main bolt about
one and a half turns. On most trucks, that will make the
truck loose enough that you can move the wheels about
a half inch or so before the pivoting action is stopped
by the rubber cushions. Tighten the lock nut after you
have the main bolt adjusted, so it will stay put.

This much "action" will allow you to make tighter,
quicker turns. Do them at a medium, fast-walk speed to
start with; try bending your knees a little to increase the
dipping motion of each turn. Turns in the direction of
your back foot work especially well this way; for example, if you ride with your right foot back and turn to the
right, you'll see that as you lean forward into the turn,
it's natural for your knees to dip and pump the board
through the turn to catch up with you. On the other
hand, when you make a *left* turn, you're forced to lean
over backwards with your knees sticking up in the air.
That's a much more awkward position for doing a snappy
little knee dip. Also, instead of tilting the board into the

illustration **37** Radical Turn

curve with your toes, you are trying to tilt it with your heels. Awkwarder and awkwarder.

To smooth out the turns to your backside, drop your behind down and a little forward, and move your back foot a bit so the toe is on the side you want to turn to, as in Illustration 36.

Somewhere along in here, before you start trying turns like the one in Illustration 37, you're going to have to loosen the main bolt again so you can use the full turning capabilities of your machine without having the thing tilt up on the edges of the wheels and go out of control. There are many different ideas as to just how loose you can set the main bolt and still have the board work right. For general sane use of a normal skateboard, however, you should only loosen it about another turn and a half from its secondary position, so it is three full turns looser than the tight way you had it at first. The outer limit of looseness will vary between different trucks, different boards, and different riders, but to me, the truck is too loose if the yoke doesn't even stay in place between the cushions, and rattles around the bolt when you ride straight. When the trucks are this loose they will be prone to "speed wobbles" a terrifying loss of control that often cannot be corrected once it starts. Loose trucks may allow the wheels to hit the underside of the board, which will be hard on the wheels and the trucks, and which will make you jerk to a stop if you're going slow. I loosen the main bolt just enough to allow me to do the sharp turns I want. If you set your wheels that way, you can make the following check to prevent the wheels-hitting-the-board problem; turn the board upside down and lay it on a flat surface, put one hand on the board so your little finger is right under the place that the wheel pivots down toward, then push that wheel down with the other hand and see if you can pinch your little finger with it until the finger hurts (see Illustration 38). If it's easy to push the wheel down and flatten your pinky, then the trucks are, in my mind, too loose. Some people may disagree with me on that point and say it's fine to have the trucks looser, but some people tear up a lot of trucks

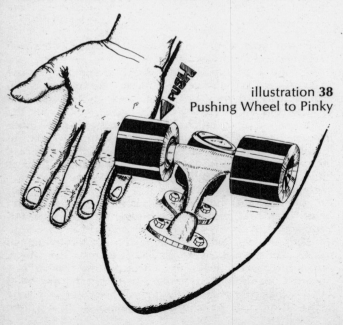

illustration 38
Pushing Wheel to Pinky

and wheels, too. For further hints on the sort of riding that may require super loose trucks, see Radical Riding, page 115. If your trucks seem *too* loose and wobbly all the time, even when you have them adjusted right, you may have cushions that are too hard; see *"Wobbly Wheels"* (page 142) for a good way to get rid of that problem.

Some people like to have the back truck a little looser than the front one. You can make it that way if you want, but it should be somewhere near the same tightness as the front truck, so do the pinky-squeezing test to make sure.

After you have both trucks adjusted the way you want them, don't forget to tighten the lock nut against the hanger plate, then leave the trucks like that. The cushions will get nice and worn in so your turning will be smooth, quick, and predictable.

Quite naturally, after you have learned how to turn fairly well and after you have gotten your skateboard adjusted right and have worked it in so you know the feel of it, you're going to be tempted to take on more challenging terrain than your gently sloping incline.

Heed a couple of warnings.

Don't skate where there's any auto traffic. Stay off crowded sidewalks. Stay off quiet private driveways, too, especially if the property owners are known to be trigger-happy shotgun toters. And the first time you set out to conquer any big hill with steep sections, start at the bottom. On foot. If you just hitch a ride to the top in a car and don't think about and study the little idiosyncrasies of pavement, gravel, steepness, and curves as you walk slowly up the hill, *before* you start hurtling down it from the top, you may find it too late to learn as you go ... faster and faster ... into the speed wobs ... through a pot-hole ... and into a long slide along that hard, rough surface that makes those big welts that don't even bleed, but just sit there glaring at you, white and SOOOOOOOOOOO painful.

Got the idea? OK, so start at the bottom of any big hill that's new to you, walk up a ways, slalom your way down, using the slowing power of traversing or "wedeling" (see page 66) to keep your speed below a fast-running pace, so you can jump off at any time. When you have gone down the lower part of the hill, walk back up it a little farther, then come winding your way down again, always staying below that point-of-no-return speed. Bite off more and more of the hill each time you walk back up, until you know how to do the whole thing without ever having to get into that fearful downhill linear accelerator trip. And while you're walking up the hill all those times, you can keep learning it better and better, so you'll be able to get the most fun out of it every time you come down.

What's that? You still itch to start at the top and just zoom right on down? Well, your head is in a different place than mine, but if your heart is set on it, at least read the Downhill Racing section in the second part of this book (page 73). DO NOT try the straight off speed runs without a special board, special experience, and special padding, or your head might wind up in a whole bunch of different places at once. I mean, can you imagine an olympic bobsled or luge racer hopping on a flexy flier at the top of a bobsled run without ever having seen the run before, and without putting on so much as a helmet? He knows he can't get the most out of any run unless he learns it by heart, slowly at first, and he also knows he will never learn anything if he goes down without a helmet and bongos his brain out in a spill. The same goes for you on your skateboard.

3
Your First Unhappy Landing

illustration 39

illustration **40**

Even if you don't have any big hills to go down where you live, or even if you're more attracted to doing the fancy footwork and tricks of flatland skateboarding rather than the risky thrills of downhill riding, sooner or later you will take some kind of fall. In fact, you'll probably take a couple of bad skids and bounces. The question is, how can you minimize the injuries from these falls? An

illustration **41** The Rolling Fall

excellent article on how to fall has been written by Jeff Campbell of the Hang Ten Skateboard Team (Skateboarder magazine, Vol. 2, No. 2). He discusses all the physics and logic behind the falls that produce broken bones, concussions, spine injuries, and massive abrasions, and he shows very clearly how to fall in such a way that you spread and absorb the impact of any fall around the more padded, fleshy parts of your body.

But the problem is that nobody likes to think about falling until it happens. And when the skateboard is no longer under you, and you are sailing through the air, you can *try* to pull Mr. Campbell's article out of your pocket and read all the laws controlling impact and the absorption of the coming collision with the ground, and then you can attempt to follow through with a graceful gymnast's roll, but you probably won't have time to get the act together and well-practiced before you hit. And when you hit everything happens so fast it's extremely hard to be unbiased and objective about how you might improve your falling technique. Usually, the first thing you get a chance to observe is all those big red strawberry patches on your arms and legs. Aaagh!

So what's to do? If you want, you can do a little falling practice. Look up the definitive Campbell article, then go

out to a lawn or into a gym with mats on the floor, and do a bunch of those rolls-out-of-the-impact which Campbell describes for forward falls, sideways falls, and backward falls; those backward falls are tricky; just try not to hit hard on your hand, elbow, or tailbone on the first bounce. You'll find that most safe falling isn't that hard to get the hang of, and the rolls can almost be fun.

If you can't be bothered with practicing such things, at least take a quick look at the simplified forward roll pictures we have put together; the forward fall is the most common, so you should at least have some idea of how to get out of that one. Then, when you fall, either forward or backward, and are in the air waiting to hit (there often *is* a split second when you think, "hey, what'm I gonna do NOW?"), don't try to remember the whole routine about falling, just think two words; "ROLL LOOSE!" When you hit, don't fight it. Just try to keep loose and rolling. It'll still be awful sometimes, but at least you'll have a chance of coming out without any badly sanded-off corners or broken Patellas.

While we're on this nasty subject, a plug must be made for some form of padding. Garden gloves are great for the hands. Heavy clothes are OK, especially in cool weather, but even better are basketball pads; they're pretty cheap, and they do a fantastic job of protecting your knees and elbows in bad falls. If you can only afford two, put them on your elbows; doctors tell me that the "skateboard fracture" of the elbow end of the humerus is the most common serious skateboard injury. If you are going to do any skating in wild terrain, get a helmet. It doesn't have to be a super-heavy motorcycle helmet; a light polo, hockey, or bicycle racer's helmet will save you in any but the worst of falls. The good thing about padding is that it not only makes skating safer, it makes you *feel* safer and more confident, so you learn faster.

In a way it's senseless to tell you all this stuff. You will learn it as it has always been learned in other sports; through many many many injuries. In the end, serious skateboarders will wear padding just as serious competitors in football and roller derby all do. But I can't help asking, why not take a short-cut and beat the crowd? Especially when the alternative is spending the rest of you life with a gimpy leg, or an achy elbow, or a tendency to drool and stumble and stare blankly at walls. Walls are for banking off, everyone knows that, so why set yourself up for a fall that'll limit you to staring at them all day?

Enough. Too much. Later with that grim stuff. Let's get on to the fun things.

illustration **42**

PART 2
Stepping Up

Introduction

Now that you have the basics down pretty well, and have learned how to fall and/or pad yourself adequately, you can start taking on some of the challenging new worlds that have been opened to the modern skateboarder by vastly improved equipment and radically new riding techniques. The following pointers and suggestions for special equipment have been drawn up to give you some ideas of the kinds of things you can try, and the kinds of skateboards you'll need in order to have a good time trying them. But do *not* consider the things I say to be the final word. I don't know how to do a quarter of the things that are humanly possible on a skateboard. And it's impossible for me to try all the thousands of new and old pieces of equipment that are now available to skateboarders. So try at all times to get the general idea of what I'm saying, and then use your own noggin to come up with the neato variations on the various techniques, and good alternatives to the equipment I suggest. The whole idea is for you to *expand* your consciousness and experience on your own, just using this book as a handy tool. There's enough pavement out there for *all* of us to fool around on. We should all dream up our own methods and equipment for doing creative things on it. After all, skateboarding isn't exclusive, like yacht sailing, where you have to sink a half million into a boat before you can set it afloat and enter a snooty race. Anybody can skateboard. And although skateboards *do* cost quite a bit more than they used to, you can get good-to-excellent equipment together if you just do a little sweating, saving, and inventing to fill the gaps that you can't fill with cash. So browse through the stuff I've come up with on the different riding styles and the different pieces of equipment, then go out and fool around a little and see if you can't come up with something better.

4
Downhill Riding

The first and most obvious thing to do with a skateboard is to ride it down a big hill. The great marvel of the modern skateboard is that you can ride it down almost any big hill, no matter how steep, without losing control and crashing. The steeper the hill, the more you traverse or "wedel" to slow yourself down. There are limits, of course, and you should do a little exploration before any big hill ride, then work out some way to get up the hill easily before you start trying out the special techniques and equipment suggested.

WHICH HILL?

If you like downhill riding, it'll be worth your while to hunt around for a nice hill. What you're looking for is a fairly wide two-lane street or road with relatively smooth pavement and little or no traffic. Dead-end streets that go back into the hills are perfect, especially if they don't have many houses along them. It's OK if the chosen street has been patched in places, as long as there aren't any big potholes or extremely rough patches of pavement. Stay away from *any* wet pavement, though; urethane loses its grip when it's wet. Hills with sudden narrow curves and blind drop-offs should be avoided too, because cars always seem to appear out of these blind spots when you least expect them. When you have found a quiet, long, traffic-free hill somewhere, take precautions so you won't lose the right to use it. Don't get in the way of any cars using the road, don't run the stop sign at the bottom, don't throw garbage around, don't vandalize the adjoining property, and don't use the roadside for a toilet. Those kinds of things make property owners grouchy. And when property owners get grouchy, skateboarders get the shaft from the local police. Now, believe me, the police don't *want* to bother with running skateboarders out of places. Really, they have much better things to do. Even in counties and cities where skateboarding is prohibited on the streets, no cop will bother you if you're on some empty dead-end where you aren't bothering anybody else. Baseball playing in the street has been prohibited for decades, after all, and the police never bust anybody for playing *that* all-American sport, as long as they stay out of the traffic. The same would be true of skateboarding, if the riders didn't do anything to aggravate the property owners, and took simple precautions like stopping before stop signs at the bottoms of their hills instead of shooting out into busy streets. Keep a low profile, in other words, and you'll keep your favorite hills much longer.

WAYS TO THE TOP

To get to your chosen hill, you can push along on your skateboard, or take a bus if one goes by your hill, or ride your bike with the skateboard attached to it by a stretch-cord, as in Illustration 43. Once you get to the bottom of the hill, you can walk up to the top; this is a good way to get up the first few times, perhaps going only part way up the first time, and studying the steep parts as you go. But once you've learned the ins and outs of a hill, you'll want some kind of a ride up. The best system is to work out a car pool with as many driving-age skateboarders as possible: that way you'll only have to drive every once in awhile. Whenever it's your turn, just drive slowly and stay way over to the side of the road so you leave plenty of room for the other guys coming down.

If you aren't in a car pool get into one before you go to the hill; going to a hill by yourself and expecting to hitch rides with some other car pool is like coming to the house of a family with eight kids at supper-time and asking for food. They won't be very obliging. If you

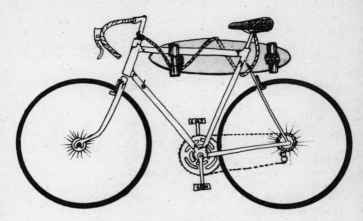

illustration **43** Board on Bike

aren't of driving age yet, save up some money and chip together with other non-drivers and pay for the car pool's gas; that'll make you a much more appreciated guest.

DOWNHILL DANCING

Every skateboarder has a different way of coming down a hill. They are all working with the same simple rhythms dictated by the road conditions, their boards, and their abilities, but it's great how they all ride differently. Try some of the following approaches for variety, then work out your own approach to your favorite hill.

When the grade is not very steep, try long, full-body-leaning turns, always aiming downhill so you don't lose much speed. Make big arcs around rough patches, see how loosely you can hold your arms as you turn, or get down in an aerodynamic squat to pick up a little speed. If you're into freestyle tricks, see if you can hold a well-balanced nose wheelie (see page 100); this might slow you down, but it passes the time while you wait for the steep sections.

When the grade gets steeper, like steeper than a one-in-eight grade, you either stop fooling around or you get locked into that linear accelerator syndrome that can lead

illustration **44**

to speed wobbles and a crash. Just what is a one-in-eight grade, you ask? Well, it means that for every eight feet you go forward, you go one foot down. It doesn't sound all that steep, I know, but it *is* steep.

If you want to get a pretty good notion of just how steep it is, or what the steepness of any portion of a hill is, use the home-made surveying technique described below, and you can not only find out how steep steep is, but you can *say* in specific terms how steep it is and remember it for comparison with other hills. Like, if you discover some fantastic new hill, and you say "Wow, it was sooooo steep, man, it was *unbelievable*," nobody will believe you. But if everybody knows a hill that is one-in-eight, and you say, "Wow, I just discovered this hill, and it's a one-in-*SIX*," they'll all know just how steep you mean. They still won't believe you, but you'll be able to prove your story by going to the new hill and doing this quick measuring method.

Steepness Measuring: Get a little torpedo level and a carpenter's square, then go to the steepest portion of your favorite local hill. Kneel somewhere near the bottom of a straight stretch and face uphill. Now set one end of the square on a fairly smooth spot on the pavement (not in a hole or on a lump) and hold it vertically, so the other end of the square points uphill. Put the level on top of the square, then tilt the square around until the bubble gets right smack in the middle of its little tube. You can steady the square in that position with one of your knees while you kneel on the other one, or lie down and hold it steady, then sight along the bottom of the level and the top of the square (see Illustration 45). Get a friend to run up the hill and put some kind of marker right at the point on the pavement where your line of sight hits. Check the level to make sure you kept the square in the right position, then check the position of the marker again. When you're sure you have marked the right place, take the level off the square. Pivot the square on the end that's down until it's lying flat on the ground with the part that was upright stretching uphill. Now count how many square-lengths there are between your starting point and the marker. If it winds up being eight, you're on a steep hill. One-in-eight grade steepness, to be exact. Well, not really too exact, but close enough to give you the idea.

There is another method of steepness testing. It's called the pit-of-the-stomach method. And although the pit of *your* stomach may not feel tight and queasy at the same steepness that *my* stomach knots up, that doesn't matter. For *you* the critical point is when *your* stomach reacts. Respect the validity of your stomach's feelings. When you feel a little twinge down in there, BACK OFF!! NOW!! Make some wide traverses, almost heading uphill during each, or do some fierce wedeling to slow you down; if the stomach-pit indicator continues to send you negative readings, turn the board straight uphill and stop. If you're already going too fast for that, head for the nearest soft

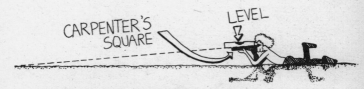

illustration **45** Measuring Steepness

dirt at the roadside and jump off. There's no rule saying you can't stop a few times during a descent, especially if you're new to the hill. As you get used to the steepness of any hill, your stomach-pit indicator will send less and less warnings to you, and you will be able to attack the hill more forcefully, and look less like a clucky-clucky going down it. But *don't* ever forget the old stomach-pit indicator. Any time it speaks up, heed it, even if all you have to do is back off for one-millionth of a second; this is the essence of being a good downhill rider of any sort. Ask a champion downhill ski racer. He'll tell you that you have to attack and attack the hill, but you must know *just* when to back off by a hair in order to keep control. And the best way to know is by how you *feel*. Downhill racers who never feel any need to back off don't last long. Especially if they are flying down paved hills instead of snow-covered ones.

The specific methods of backing off are the wide traverse and the fast wedel. Traversing is pretty simple, and doesn't require much more explanation than Illustration 46. Just make more and more traverses as the hill gets steeper and steeper, and straighten out more as you come to flat areas.

Wedeling is more challenging. The word means "tail-wagging" in German; it is borrowed from alpine ski terminology, and refers to the way a good skier can start at the top of almost any hill, no matter how steep, and go straight down, controlling his speed by the use of short, tail-wagging, slide-slipping turns which he does

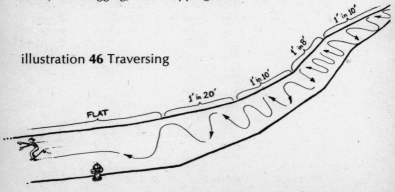

illustration **46** Traversing

with his skis parallel and the upper part of his body facing downhill all the time. In skateboarding, the same sort of rapid side-slipping turns can be used as brakes, but the rider must have excellent control over his board to keep from either spinning out or gaining too much speed to be able to keep in rhythm. Practice wedeling on a *short* steep hill to start with, so that if the speed gets away from you, you can straighten off and coast to the bottom without accelerating up to the speed where the wobbles set in. To get the feel of the breaking-loose point of your wheels on the particular pavement you're riding, try some wide, swooping turns and traverses, taking each one a little faster until you drift sideways ever so slightly. That's the type of minimal slide you want to do quickly and accurately as you wedel. It is essential that you balance your weight carefully in any side-slipping move. If you aren't pushing *down* on the nose and the tail of the board at the same time that you are pushing it *sideways* through the turn, the unweighted end of the board will slide, spin out, and make you fall. When you are making a turn toward the side of your front foot, like a left turn if you ride left-foot-forward, the tendency will be to lean on your back foot and unweight the front wheels, allowing them to skid straight

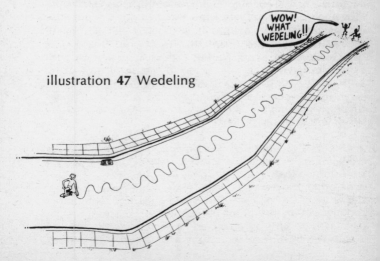

illustration **47** Wedeling

instead of through a corner. In turns to the opposite side of your front foot you'll tend to lean on the *front* foot so the back wheels get unweighted, slide, and spin out. You want a slight four-wheel drift to slow you down; you don't want to go into a wild slide and slow down by hitting the pavement.

Different riders with different sorts of boards do different things to control the fore-and-aft balance problem. A light rider with a short, stiff board will have to put his feet pretty much over the two trucks, and he'll have to do a lot of work and maybe even some arm-flapping to keep the sideways drift smooth. A heavy rider on a longer board can place his feet far apart, almost over the trucks, like the sort board rider, and then use his weight and the long area over which it is distributed to get nice big sweeping slide-turns. Surfers tend to favor this sort of turn because it is similar to what they do on their surfboards. A third option for riders who have medium-to-long boards with some flex and "twang" or resiliency is to stand with their feet close together in the middle of the board, or forward of the middle, and to control the drift by the way they lean and bend their knees. It seems hard at first, but if you learn to control this board-bending type of turn, you'll see that it often makes smoother wedeling style than the wide stance. It lets the board act as a shock absorber to even out irregularities of pavement and traction. It also takes full advantage of the twang of the board (in the case of boards like the Gordon and Smith Fibreflex, this twang can be considerable), giving the rider a terrific sense of flow as he bobs and swoops down a steep hill like a champion skier in powder snow. You can even push your knees together for stability like skiers do. It looks soooo classy when you do it right!

One you've mastered the slowing-down technique of wedeling, you can mix it in with traverses, some power-slide turns (see page 98), riding in a crouch, and whatever other moves you want to decorate your downhill dance with. Or you can concentrate on slalom techniques, picking out marks or pieces of dirt or patches on the pavement to use as imaginary gate markers as you go along. The mixture of wide turns and carefully controlled slides is essential in this game; if, for instance, you have to make a wide turn on a steep hill to get around a particular set of marks, and you want to keep your speed in the controllable range as you do the wide turn, you'll have to pull two really fast wedel turns in the middle of the wide turn, as shown in Illustration 48. Many riders call this a "check turn," because of its similarity to a surfing turn.

On the more level portions of a hill, like those that are about one-in-twenty, you can coast in gentle curves as in Illustration 46, but you can also do a sort of reverse wedeling, known as pumping. Pumping requires a board with some twang and a rider who can use his body english in perfect rhythm with the board as it turns and flexes. If you weight and unweight the board at just the right moments, and twist in such a way that you "pull" the board through each turn, it will actually accelerate as it goes weaving along. Don't let the wheels slide at all while pumping, or you'll lose speed. Some people find it easier to learn this trick on flat land at slow speeds (see page 95), but you can learn it while moving at a good clip, too.

Some other downhill entertainments include dotted white line slaloming (to be done only on deserted streets with no blind corners), zooming up and down steep drive-

illustration **48** Check Turn

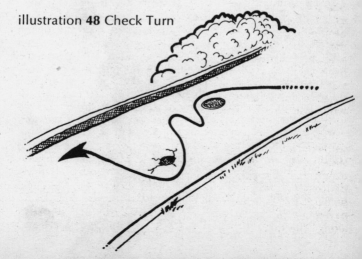

ways that join the road (watch for grumpy property
owners), riding in a line holding hands, and informal
dogfights among several riders who buzz in and out
among each other like choreographed biplane pilots. Do
these last two games on hills that are one-in-twelve or
less steep, and do them with riders who are all of fairly
even ability.

Every road has its own character. Try any of the things
mentioned above that seem to fit, or work out new stunts
for special situations. Like if there's a smoothly paved
gutter with a high lip, try banking off it, or if you spot a
squirrel wandering out into the road, give chase. Whatever works.

SLALOM

If you want to develop your downhill turning style to
the ultimate degree of precision and speed, take up the
serious side of downhill dancing, the slalom. You can set
up a slalom on any hill, or even on the flat if you want
to include pumping or pushing along with your foot to
keep up speed. In competition, though, the slalom course
is usually laid out on a hill with a grade of about one-
in-nine or one-in-ten, with a short flat stretch at the end;
the competitors must have both feet on their boards
going through the first gate, and they must keep their
feet on their boards all the way through the course and
across the finish line. To set up a coarse like one of the
ones in Illustration 49, you can get traffic safety cones
for gate markers, but if that's too much hassle, you can
make markers out of a bunch of six ounce paper cups
and rubber balls that you stuff into the cups to keep them
from blowing away in the wind. Set up the course near
the bottom of a grade, so you have a flat stretch as well
as the incline gates. Mark the spot on the pavement
where you set each cone or cup with a chalk "X" so
you can replace the marker if it gets knocked over. The
gates can be set in a straight line, 12–15 feet apart, for
a start. Then, as you get better, you can move alternate
markers to one side, or even make a meandering course
like the one on the right in Illustration 49, in order to
make it difficult to get the precise turning rhythm required to go through the course at top speed without
spinning out, hitting a gate, or falling.

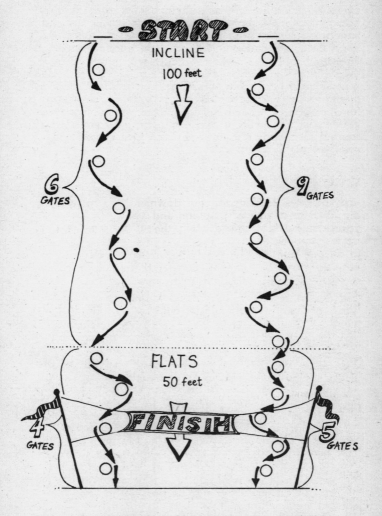

- START -

INCLINE

100 feet

6 GATES

9 GATES

FLATS

50 feet

4 GATES

FINISH

5 GATES

illustration **49** An Easy Slalom and a Harder Slalom

illustration **50** A Friendly Sunday Race

Different people like different kinds of slalom challenges. Those who enjoy skateboarding at the ragged edge of control and traction will want to move their course to a very steep grade, like a one-in-eight, which will make it a real tough proposition just to stay on the course. The fun of a steep course is the mastery of all that gravity-energy that wants to push you out of the gates and into the old linear accelerator going straight downhill. You will have to do lots of four-wheel drifting in the turns, and your timing will be extremely critical.

For those who get a kick out of working for precision at more manageable speeds, the slalom can be set on a grade of one-in-ten or even less, and made more difficult by putting the gates closer together and in erratic patterns, so the skateboarder has to work hard to keep up speed. In this sort of course, the object is to use up as *little* of the gravity-energy as possible in your turns, so that momentum will be kept up through the finish flat. Where the steep slalom rider uses the controlled slides of wedeling, the gradual-incline slalom rider will try to keep his wheels from sliding, and he will do some vigorous pumping in his turns to increase his speed

right up to just below the sliding speed. It takes not
only the control and timing that's necessary for steep
slaloming, but also the coordinated use of body english
and perfect aim to cut the gates as close as possible. It's
much more ·difficult than it looks, and although not as
spectacular as the steep slalom, often graceful and dance-
like.

DOWNHILL RACING

This form of skateboard riding is for speed and speed
only. The general idea is to find a very steep, straight,
well-paved, traffic-free road, and to start at the top and
come right on down as fast as you can go. But that's
only the general idea. If you or I were to do that on our
normal boards and with our lack of racing experience,
we would either be uncompetitively slow (if the hill were
not very steep) or so fast and wobbly that we would
lose grip and splatter all over. Good downhill racers
work their way up to the high-speed trip after years of
flatland riding, slaloms, and slower downhill riding. They
master all of the different skateboard techniques *before*
they begin their racing. It may not look like those guys
are doing all that much at high speed, but believe me,
they *are*.

The danger of downhill racing is, in fact, the very
simplicity of it. All it takes is for you to see some hot-
shot come whooshing down the hill, frozen in a streamlined squat or maybe even prone on his board, and you
will be tempted to say "Gee, that doesn't look so hard;
he's just sitting there, cruising along at thirty-five or forty
without batting an eye; all I'd have to do is tighten up
my trucks a little, and I could go as fast if not faster."
And up to about twenty or maybe even twenty-five miles
per hour, you'd do fine, squatting down on your normal
board with its tight trucks and tucking your helmetless
head under one unpadded elbow. But then you might
start to wobble, or drift a little, or drift *and* wobble, and
then you would wish you had worked your way up to
downhill racing instead of jumping right into it. But it
would be too late.

So if you want to get the feel of speed, do a little 20 mph run on a short hill with the trucks on your board tightened up on the cushions; wear a <u>helmet</u>, <u>gloves</u>, and <u>knee and elbow pads</u>, and you won't get hurt badly even if you get the wobs and take a spill. But don't try the higher speeds until you have been skateboarding so long that you have *absolute* confidence, both in yourself and in your carefully prepared board. There is *no* room for error at high speed, and the steadiness of the rider must be monumental to overcome the inherent unsteadiness of the machine and the surfaces it flies along with its tiny little wheels turning at something like 8,000 rpm. Yeah, I worked it out; that's how fast they're going around when the board is traveling at fifty miles per hour. You better be sure you're ready for the sorts of vibrations that get going at that speed. The main thing needed is control; steel nerves, iron muscles, and an uncrackable will. But those aren't things you can buy in a store or build up overnight, so it's best to leave the speed racing to the old pros until you have been skateboarding long enough to think of yourself as one. By that time you may decide that searching for the terminal velocity of a skateboard is a little silly. I mean, the surest way to set the unbreakable record is to jump off a bridge hanging onto a skateboard and put yourself into a streamlined position. But what's the point? I like to *feel* like I'm going fast, and I feel that way most intensely when I'm going fifteen miles per hour around a turn that I should only go through at ten. Hurtling down some near-vertical descent in a full leather suit would make me feel *fear* and not much else. If that's your idea of fun, OK; just make sure you are experienced enough to do it properly and with a minimum of risk.

DOWNHILL EQUIPMENT

You can ride safely down almost any hill, even if it is a one-in-seven grade, using the equipment described in the First Board chapter. All you need is good urethane wheels and a thorough mastery of the various slowing-down techniques. But if downhill riding gets under your skin and you develop specific tastes for one type of riding or another, you might want to try some more refined equipment.

Wheels: For downhill dancing, where you aren't trying to set any speed records, you need a wheel that will last long under rough treatment and have good traction and a gradual break into slides so you can do wedeling, traversing, or full-on sliding all without loosing control or wearing your wheels out every few weeks. Road Riders will work very well for this kind of riding. They stretch and grip the road like no other wheels; they last long, break smoothly and slowly into slides, and roll fairly fast, too. There are other wheels, particularly large ones like the Roller Sports Stoker and the large Power Paws, and even the huge Sims wheel, that have fair-to-good traction, good-to-excellent speed, and the ability to break slowly into slides, but these wheels are too big to use with normal trucks and a standard board like your first one. See *"Trucks"* and *"Board Tops"* (below) for possible alterations to provide extra clearance.

For slalom you need wheels that have good traction but that also deliver the highest speed possible. Larger diameter wheels have less rolling resistance and are therefore often better. The small Road Riders are not as fast as other larger wheels, like the large Road Riders (which haven't the traction of the small wheels), or the Roller Sports Big Wheels or the large Sims wheels or the Bennett Alligator Wheels. There is some disagreement among slalom riders about how these different wheels work and which is fastest, and there are some riders who like other new wheels, but almost all competition is done on larger diameter wheels than the ones recommended for the standard trucks and boards. If you move up to large wheels for slalom, you should do the necessary changes of equipment described under *"Trucks"* and *"Board Tops"* below.

When trying to decide which wheel will be the fastest for any type of slalom, don't just consider size, however. Some larger wheels are slower because their great width makes them have more rolling resistance. In *general*, increased diameter makes for a faster wheel with less traction, while increased width decreases speed and increases traction.

Hardness and softness affect the wheel too. Hard wheels often don't have very good traction, and if the road surface is bumpy they aren't even as fast as softer wheels. But softness isn't a simple characteristic either. Two wheels that are of the same softness can react differently; this is because some types of urethane get "mushy" or more viscous as they are made softer, while others get more bouncy or elastic. Bouncy urethane takes care of the unevenness of the road surface more easily than mushy urethane and therefore goes faster; to get the idea of a bouncy urethane wheel, drop a Road Rider on a hard surface.

The design of a wheel, the shapes of its inner and outer walls and the placement of the bearings, can also affect the wheel's speed and traction, so they must be considered too.

All these considerations make the choice of a slalom wheel a complicated process. Try different wheels out. Ask around about the performance of different wheels before you buy. Then try to get the wheel that suits your style, rather than the wheel that is most popular or newest at the moment.*

For downhill racing you'll need wheels that are not only large in diameter but harder than normal, to lower rolling resistance. Wheels with hard cores seem to be the fastest, especially on smooth pavement. Needless to say, these wheels are prone to slides, and must only be used when they are still fairly new, and even then only by a rider who knows exactly what their limitations are at speed.

Trucks: Sure Grip and other decent, inexpensive trucks will do fine for downhill skating with good standard sized

---

* A number of large wheels have appeared on the market, and a few extra wide ones as well. Although these special-size wheels are good for some special purposes, they often have drawbacks. The wide ones are slow unless they are made of hard urethane. The large diameter ones tend to have poor traction, and you often need to alter the board and add risers to get adequate clearance for sharp turns. Get the large or wide wheels only if you have a special need and are willing to do the alterations for them. One trick which improves the traction of the large wheels, especially those made of good urethane, is to ride them hard on a rough street surface; do controlled slides at low speed and you'll notice that little "ruffles" soon get built up on the surface of each wheel. These ruffles act like tire treads and make the wheels grip better.

wheels; they'll do especially well if you get soft cushions for them (see page 143). But if you try to put tall or wide wheels on them for speed and/or traction, the first time you take a sharp corner you will notice that the wheels hit the bottom of the board. To remedy this situation, you can do one of three things; you can elevate the board by inserting risers (or "shock pads" as they are sometimes called) between the trucks and the board top, or you can get special high trucks (like the Bennett Hijackers or the Dick Brewer trucks), or you can just alter the shape of the board top to make more clearance (see "Board Tops," below).

The trouble with elevating the board is that it raises the point where all your weight is balancing above the wheels. The higher this point is, the more you have to shift your weight and the position of your feet on the board in order to turn. There is one way you can raise the board up over big wheels and get a fantastically solid ride, but it costs lots. The way is called Tracker Trucks. These trucks are made big and superstrong, and they are easy to adjust, and they are extremely wide (six and three-quarters inches to be exact), and they are famous for their smooth, controllable turning action; when you crank into a tight turn with Trackers the wheels break loose one at a time because of the fact that the ones on the outer side of the turn are so much farther out that they are going faster than the inside wheels. It makes for a luscious spreading-warm-butter sort of a feeling as you drift with perfect control through almost any turn. It makes wedeling a cinch; it also makes it easy to avoid sliding and keep good control for slaloming, even if you *do* have to raise the board up at least a half inch to get wheel clearance. The Tracker trucks are very expensive, though; other less expensive trucks with a lot of width have appeared, such as the California Slalom and the slightly narrower and heavier steel Continental. These newer trucks, though they aren't as easy to adjust, both have main bolt arrangements that are less prone to bottoming-out damage than the special Tracker set-up, so you should consider them as alternatives if you don't mind getting either a little extra weight (on the steel trucks) or slightly weaker construction; unless you are very competitive or very hard on your trucks, they will all hold up fine.

The Bennett Hijacker trucks have solved both the wheel and the main bolt clearance problems, but to get all that clearance, it has been necessary to change the geometry of the truck. The axle has been moved down and toward the end of the board from the pivot and the yoke, a change that makes the steering more sensitive than usual. The soft, pliant cushions on Bennett trucks increase the effect of the sensitive steering. This is great if you want to do many tight turns at low speed, but for faster slalom or downhill dancing action, it can tend to get a little squirrely. Some people can get used to the light touch of the Bennett trucks and use it to good advantage, but it takes some real doing.

Trucks for downhill racing need not be high or wide. They need only be stiff. No loose pivot, no loose cushions, no shilly-shallying around at all. There are people who use trucks with loose cushions for downhill racing, but I think that's tempting fate. You can use your standard trucks and your first board if they are both stiff and stable. If your trucks have soft cushions, you might want to change to harder urethane ones. And before every speed run, make sure every nut and bolt on the board is rock solid tight.

BOARD TOPS

You can choose the board that fits your style and taste in downhill riding after you've had some experience on your first board.

If you like big sweeping turns and are willing to move around on the board a little for effective wedeling and sharp turns, you can try one of the long boards. They range in length from thirty to fifty inches, and are most often made of high-quality hardwood like birch and long-grained ash. They are usually 9/16" to 3/4" thick, so that they are plenty strong enough, even if there are channels or grooves cut in them for wheel clearance. If you are pretty heavy (like over 125 pounds), you will be able to flex a longer board a little in turns, thus lowering your center of gravity nicely between the wheels, even if you have to use a 1/4" or 1/2" riser for wheel clearance. You can do a lot more stunting around on these big boards than you might think; you ought to see Tom Sims or

Bruce Logan, two good riders and makers of different types of wood boards; they can do all kinds of stunts on wood boards, and Tom Sims often uses one of his ash boards that's over four feet long. If you want a big wood board; it's best to get a blank from a good maker like Sims or Logan, rather than making your own big wood top; a lot of know-how and care goes into the selection, cutting, and shaping of a big wood board to insure that it will be strong enough in the right places. But if you get one and find that your big downhill wheels hit the board in sharp turns, you can avoid using big risers by cutting wheel-wells into the wood with a router (don't cut them any deeper than necessary) or cutting channels in from the edges with a Stanley Surform shaping tool like the one shown in Illustration 51. If you get carried away doing this channeling, and make gaping U-shaped holes that might weaken the board, you can inset top plates of thin birch plywood, as described on pages 84–85. If you like to do lots of wheelies, kick-turns, and rotation stunts on your big wood board (they look flashy with that big ironing board waving around), you'll tear up the tail of the board rapidly. To prevent

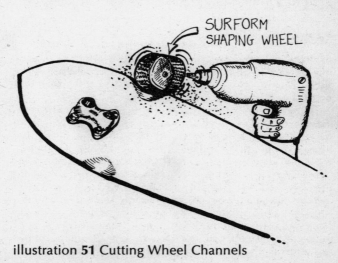

SURFORM
SHAPING WHEEL

illustration 51 Cutting Wheel Channels

this or at least slow it down, put a tail-saver made out of hard-rock maple on the back of your board, or glue and nail a big shoe tap back there, or install a neato Kevin Reed tail-saver; all of these gizmos are explained under *"Tail Dragging"* on page 156.

At the opposite extreme from the big indestructible power-turning downhill board is the small, flexible, sensitive board. These usually measure only about six to eight inches longer than your stance length (see Illustration 2), and they will suit the rider who is interested in precision turning rather than the big powerful moves at high speeds. Pultruded fiberglass boards with a little flex to them and the super-flexy-twangy Gordon and Smith fibreflex boards (which use archery bow lamination technology) dominate the small slalom board field at the moment. Other special laminated boards are beginning to appear, and there will probably be exciting new developments in this area. Also, there are some often-overlooked plastic boards in this size range that work very well if you have a taste for them. The higher-quality polypropelene boards, though they aren't twangy, have been proven very usable by some hot slalom riders who don't *like* the springboard feel of the twangy boards. Lexan boards like the Roller Sports Pro-line are another good, semi-twangy possibility, as are the fiberglass-strengthened nylon boards like those made of Dupont Zytel. The only trouble with all these alternate plastic boards is that they are thicker and often a little more sluggish and heavy than the fiberglass and laminated boards.

Two types of commercially-produced boards which do *not* seem to work well for slalom are the acrylic (lucite or plexiglass, for instance) boards, and the aluminum ones. Acrylic plastics get brittle in sunlight and chip, crack, or break in half, even if they are laminated. Aluminum is OK if it is of very high quality, and thick enough, like 3/16" (.190") 2024 T4 or T6, or 7075 T6, for instance. But boards made out of high-grade treated aluminum like that are rare and expensive. Many boards are made out of the softer aluminum types, like 6061, which is much less resilient and which will lose its memory and sag after awhile if you are hard on it. The worst trouble with aluminum boards is that they don't say right on

them what kind of aluminum they are made of, and re-
tailers often don't know. It isn't worth the expense unless
you know you're getting the highest grade of aluminum,
so I don't recommend getting aluminum boards for
slalom at all. It's too bad, because there *are* boards made
of aluminum that work beautifully, and which dampen
road shocks much more than fiberglass does, producing
a smoother ride.

If you haven't got the money for one of the fancy
short and sensitive slalom boards, and you want to save
up for the fancy trucks and wheels, you can just make
your own board, either out of plywood and fiberglass,
or out of very high-grade hardwood and thin birch ply.

Home-made Slalom Boards: For a short and flexy (but
not too twangy or resilent) board that can be made in
a single afternoon and used the next day, get the best
quality 3/8" plywood you can find, like marine-grade
mahogany, or (if you can find it) 5-ply finish birch like
they use in cabinets and for aircraft construction. Cut
out a pattern like one of those in the First Board chapter
(page 11) or make a slim design for wide wheel clearance
by tracing around one of the fancy thin-nose, thin-tail
slalom boards like the Gordon and Smith or Ty Page units.
Cut out the wood with a coping saw, a jig saw, a band
saw, or a saber saw, whichever you can get ahold of.
File and sand the rails (edges) of the board until they are
round, smooth, and splinter-free. Draw a clear, dark
center line and truck placement lines on the bottom of
the board (see Illustration 24), then buy a six inch wide
strip of eight ounce fiberglass patching cloth that is about
six feet long, or a 12" × 36" rectangle, and a pint of

3/8" PLYWOOD   8 OZ. FIBERGLASS

illustration **52** Plywood Sandwich Board

epoxy or polyester resin. Cut out two pieces of fiberglass (use a sharp pair of scissors; that stuff can be the dickens to cut evenly without fraying). Make pieces the same shape as the board, but smaller, so there will be about ½" between the edge of the glass and the edge of the board. Mix up about half of the resin and half of the hardening catalyst in a clean can or metal bowl that you are prepared to throw away if it gets ruined. When the resin is thoroughly mixed, use a throw-away paint brush to apply it over the piece of fiberglass on the top of the board (the side that has no placement lines on it). Apply a light coat, making sure it soaks through the glass cloth all over and leaves no bubbles, but also making sure not to put it on too thick in any one place. When you have a nice thin coat that allows the texture of the glass cloth to show, and that won't drip, turn the board over and clamp it in a vise bottom up. Put the other piece of glass cloth on what will be the bottom of the board, then pour and paint a thick layer of resin on this side, a layer that's thick enough to cover all the texture of the cloth. Try to keep the resin from slopping and dripping over the sides of the board at all times; you'll just have to sand that slop off later. Work quickly as you brush the resin to a smooth surface, or the stuff will "set up" (harden) before you've had a chance to finish spreading it and cleaning it off your hands. If you are fast you can clean off with a lot of laundry detergent or Boraxo, vigorously applied: if you're too slow and some of the resin hardens on your hands or under your fingernails (youch, it stings under there, doesn't it?)), you can get a little Acetone to clean it off. But WATCH IT!! Acetone is potent stuff. It'll clean your skin off just as readily as it cleans the resin off (ack! and you thought that resin hurt under your fingernails!). When you are finished with the resin and the Acetone, wash your hands throughly with mild soap and lots of water to get rid of all the vile chemicals. Once the glass is thoroughly hard (you should wait overnight to make sure), place the hanger plates along their placement lines. You can put them near the ends of the board, like on the hot-shot slalom boards. That will give you more clearance for wide wheels and a longer wheelbase for stability and maximum flex.

Drill the 5/32" guide holes through the board from the bottom, using the hanger plates for exact placement, as in the First Board chapter (Chapter 1). Then use a counter-sinking bit to make the nice little sinks in the glass deck of the board for the heads of 8-32 flat head machine screws. As you do the counter-sinking check the depth of each sink often by turning the screw head down and seeing if the hole is as wide as the head; take it slow; if the sink gets too wide and deep, the screw will pull down through the glass and into the board, thus weakening it. Get 8-32 screws that are just long enough to go through the board, the hanger plates, the nut, and what-ever risers you have to use to get wheel clearance (if you have Tracker trucks, use 12-24 machine screws and drill 3/16" guide holes). On short boards, I think you should keep the risers to a minimum, because the wheels are closer together than on a big board, and the higher you go, the poorer your stability is. This problem is minimized if you use a thin-nose-and-tail shape and put wide trucks near the ends of your slalom board. When you have mounted your hanger plates, trucks, and wheels on your new board (see pages 21–40 for help if you need it) check to make sure you have enough clearance for the wheels in a sharp turn. If there is not enough, you can cut channels into the rails with a Surform tool, as de-scribed on page 79. That's the nice thing about the Ply-wood and fiberglass sandwich board; it leaves the rails free of fiberglass so you can work on them, and so they will not chip, fray and get sharp when you drag them or bang them into things. The more expensive boards with glass all around them get very sharp, ragged, and ugly around the edges. Your homemade board will look better and be safer to ride, too, especially if you file and sand down any splintery holes caused by bang-ups.

The plywood sandwich board can also be made out of ¼" thick high-grade plywood (like 5-ply birch, for instance); you just have to use *three* layers of glass cloth on each side for strength. These thinner boards are light, twangy, and good-looking at first, but after awhile they tend to get saggy. They often break after about six months of heavy use, too, but if you don't mind making them, you can just do that every time you use one up.

Another way to make an elegant board of your own, a board on which you can control the amount of flex and twang as you build it, is to hunt around and find a piece of super-good hardwood and make a thin, laminated-ended board out of it. It takes a little leg-work finding well-seasoned wood, and it takes some time, effort, and borrowed tools to get the board made, but it will not only be flexy and twangy when you get done with it, it will also be super-strong and good-looking.

If you can find some air-dried hickory for your board, you are in luck. This wood used to be used for archery bows, and they still make sledge-hammer handles out of it; it is fantastically strong and twangy. Kiln-dried hickory, which is more common because it is used for flooring, will work if you get a piece with minimal run-out and close grain like the wood in Illustration 6. Close and straight-grained white oak will do, too, if you don't weigh over 150 pounds. Straight-grained birch and ash are fine, too, although they are a little less twangy. Whichever wood you find, get a piece that's ⅜" or ½" × 8", and however long you need. It will cost you about three to five bucks. How's that compare to the price of a Gordon and Smith Fibreflex board top?

If you get ½" stock or even 1" stock from the lumber yard (sometimes they don't carry anything thinner), you'll have to get it machine-planed down to ⅜" at your school or boy's club shop or at a local cabinet shop or mill; hand-planing hardwoods is grueling work, to say the least. For any board except the longest (over 36 inches), and for any rider except the heaviest (over 175 pounds), you want to have the board ⅜" thick or just a hair thinner. If the wood has a lot of run-out, however, as the example in Illustration 1, it should be at least ½" thick to prevent breakage.

When you have your chosen piece of high-class hard-wood, all planed down and pretty, make a cardboard template for it, either using the patterns on page 11, or tracing the shape of a slim-ended slalom board like the Gordon and Smith or the Ty Page. Trace the outline of your board from the template onto the hardwood, but DON'T CUT IT OUT YET!! While you still have a rec-tangular piece of wood, mark a center line on what will be the bottom, then draw placement lines; if the trucks are going to be big wide ones, you can put them near the ends of your thin-nose-and-tail board, and get a lot of wheel clearance and stability. Trace the outline of the trucks on the wood when you have them where you want them, then make marks on the edge of the board where the front and back of each truck is, as in Illustration 53. Now measure ½" out from each mark on the edge of the board and make marks showing how wide the top plates are going to be, as shown. Take a square and mark straight lines across the top of the board for the edges of the plate slots, then go to your school or boy's club or friendly neighbor's wood shop and set a table saw VERY carefully so the blade sticks up ⅛" and *no* more. That ain't much. Take a scrap of wood and check to make sure the saw cuts a groove that's just ⅛" deep when you shove it over the blade (careful now; even if the blade is only sticking up a little, it can still take one of your fingers off). When you have the saw adjusted to cut ⅛" grooves, get the sliding miter gauge (the pusher thing that has a protractor you can set to cut at different angles) set at exactly ninety degrees. Push your board top over the saw again and again, moving it about ⅛" to the side each time, until you have cut out the top plate slots between your lines as in Illustration 53. It's all right if there are some little lumps and burrs sticking up when you finish sawing; you can file off the ones that stick up a lot, and leave a slightly rough surface, which will make the laminating glue stick even better than a smooth surface would.

The *only* material to use for the truck mounting plates is ⅛" five ply birch plywood. FIVE plies in ⅛"! Wow.

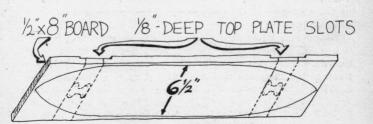

illustration **53** Top Plate Placement

That's unreal, isn't it? It's a great building material. Supposed to be about the strongest sheet material, pound for pound, in the world. Good old mother nature, coupled with a yankee ingenuity for lamination. You can get small sheets of this wonderfully strong plywood at hobby shops; they use it for making model boats and planes. If you buy two 6" × 12" sheets, they'll take care of the four truck plates you need. If you can't find a hobby shop that has birch plywood, you can write to the best maker of the stuff for a catalogue (write to Sig Manufacturing Company, Montezuma, Iowa). Cut the top plates a tiny bit large at first, then file the edges down to fit the slots snugly. If the plates stick up a little instead of fitting flush, you can file the slots down near the corners to get a good flush fit.

Cut two 4" × 6" pieces of birch-ply for the two bottom truck plates. Make the shape for these plates by centering a truck hanger, or a riser, whichever will be mounted there, on the plate; copy the outline of the hanger or riser, then draw diagonal lines from about halfway out on the outline off to the edge of the plate, so you wind up with the funny shape like the ones in Illustration 54. That shape is a pain to cut out, I know; use a jig saw or a band saw. It will make it easier to cut wheel clearance channels if you need to later; it also spreads out the stress on the bottom of the board so it won't break. Before you do any gluing, clamp the plates in place, put the whole board in a vice, center the truck hangers where you want them (near the ends if you want wheel clearance on a narrow board), and drill all the 5/32" guide

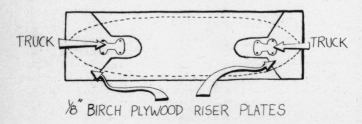

illustration **54** Riser Plates

holes through the truck hangers, the risers (if you are
using any), the birch ply, and the board itself. See page
24 if you need hints on how to do the hanger plate placement and guide hole drilling. Turn the board over and
counter-sink the holes in the top plates for the heads of
the 8-32 machine screws (if you are putting Tracker
trucks on your board, you can use big strong 12-24
machine screws, for which you have to drill large 3/16"
guide holes). Run the bit you used through each hole a
bunch of times so the machine screws will slide through
easily.

Now you can unclamp the board and take everything
apart. Spread good glue on the plates for lamination.
Elmer's Glue-all will do, but Weldwood or aliphatic resin
type glue like Titebond, which is used for wood models,
will be the best. Put the well-glued plates into place on
the board and in the slots, push the machine screws
through everything, including the hanger plates, and
tighten them down as hard as they'll go (see the Big
Cinch-down, page 25, for help). If you can get four C-
clamps or gluing clamps, clamp the plates near the rails
of the board to make double sure you have a good solid
lamination all the way across.

After the glue is dry, you can cut out the pattern of
the board with a coping saw, a jig saw, a band saw, or
a saber saw, whichever you can get ahold of. Cut slowly
so you don't tear up the plywood of the truck plates.
Then plane, file, and finally sand the rails until they are
round and as smooth as a baby's bottom. You'll notice
that the edges of the truck plates show their layers clearly
if you shape them right. It looks classy. And for such a
decent price. Mount your trucks and wheels (see page
21–32 for help) when the board has a nice smooth surface, and you can try the thing out.

If the wheels don't have quite enough clearance when
you're done, you can cut channels for them with a Surform tool (see page 79); you won't have to worry about
lessening the strength of the board because of the fact
that it is sandwiched between those super-strong laminations of birch-ply. If the board isn't quite flexy enough
for you, plane or use a belt sander to take a bit off the
deck. Don't take too much, though. Don't take any at
all off the bottom of the board, either, because it will

break in as you use it, and if you weaken the bottom (which takes the greatest strain as the board flexes) the board may get saggy or even split.

As a finishing touch, put strips of non-slip tape on the deck (as in Illustration 26). Hardwood boards tend to get slick on top with use, so you'll need that extra traction. When the board is all just the way you want it, rub a linseed oil mixture (one part linseed oil mixed with two parts paint thinner) into the wood with a rag. It'll bring out the grain beautifully, and prevent warping and "checking" or cracking. Do a linseed and thinner rub on your masterpiece once every month or so and it will last for years.

The long wood board tops and short homemade boards discussed above will work just fine for most kinds of downhill dancing, fast slalom, and slower precision slalom racing. For the speed fanatic who wants a board for Downhill Racing, the main quality to stress is *stability*. Some downhill racers can be most stable on a short (24"–27") stiff fiberglass board. Others feel that a longer board with just a little flex is better because it will soak up some of the shocks that come from the road. Thin shock-absorbing rubber risers are used on many high-speed boards for this same reason, but they should not be so soft that they squish out of shape and get loose. Find out what works for you when you're going fast. Whichever way you go, you should have *absolute* faith in your board, so either get a first-rate pultruded fiberglass top, or get a long wood or laminated board made by someone who is an *expert* in the field. Don't tempt the fates with a poorly made or weak board. You needn't do any channeling or put in any big risers on a racing board, because you'll never be turning sharply. Place the trucks near to the ends of the board, though, for maximum stability.

A Warm Day at Frederick

Little Ian "Kneeing" at Frederick

Tim Piumarta

Tim Piumarta

John Hudson—Fluid Slalom

Terry Brown

8

5
Flatland Freestyle Riding

Not everyone has a hill right nearby where he can go downhill skateboarding. And some of you may not be able to get rides to the hills, even if there are some in your area. And still others of you many not *like* looking down a one-in-seven grade from the top, and knowing that the only thing keeping you from sure destruction is your ability to traverse and wedel effectively. For all those kinds of people man has created endless thousands of acres of flat and gently sloping pavement, in the form of empty parking lots, broad sidewalks, dead-end streets, driveways, bike paths, basketball and tennis courts, and backyard patios. Any of these places can become your practice area or your performance stage, as long as nobody else wants to use the pavement for something more urgent. To keep skateboarding from being prohibited in all of the nice flatland places, be courteous and move over or stop riding when a car, pedestrian, or bicycle needs to go by. And keep away from places where other activities like basketball games and tennis matches are in progress. That way, skateboarding will be allowed the same way other informal games are allowed on quiet streets, parking lots, and other places out of people's way. If skateboarding is illegal where you live, make *double* sure you stay out of any situation where you bother anybody; do it like the neighborhood baseball players who have been playing on empty streets for decades, even though it is technically illegal; you'll find that respect for other people's needs can make it possible to skateboard even in the most anti-skateboard communities.

When you have found a nice secluded and trafficless place to do your flatland freestyle skateboarding, make sure the surface is free of water, pebbles, and sand. If water is standing on the pavement, don't take any chances riding through it; urethane has poor gripping power when it gets wet, and it doesn't give any warning before it breaks loose and slides, so you tend to go down in the puddle before you know what's happening. If there are just a couple pebbles sitting around on the pavement where you want to do freestyle skateboarding, pick them up and throw them out of the way, but if there are many pebbles and/or little patches of gravel, leaves, or sand, it's worth the trouble to get a push-broom and sweep the area clean; all it takes is one pebble in the wrong place when you're in the middle of a three-sixty or a handstand or something, and the wheel will stop and you'll go down.

When your chosen freestyle spot is clean enough to fool around on, the only limits to what you can do are your ability and your imagination. The following tricks are *not* meant to be the best ones, or the only ones the hot-shots do, or even the best ones for you to perform. They are just a few basic stunts, shown mostly to give you an idea of how many different sorts of things you can do on a skateboard. Once you have mastered some of these tricks, you should definitely forget all about learning what this book or anybody else tells you to learn. Make up your own tricks; originality is much more fun, and if you ever want to get into competition, the judges will be looking for that originality as well as ability and style. *Propulsion:* To get moving on the flatland, you can always do a little pushing along with your foot, and it might even be a good idea to learn how to alternate feet if you're going to travel any distance on level terrain. But you can develop two other forms of propulsion that don't require taking either foot off the board. The first is pumping, a sort of reverse wedeling, as described on page 69. At slow speeds it is done best by means of precisely timed twisting motions of the upper body that "pull" the board through the turns, increasing speed just a bit at a time. At higher speeds you can throw your whole body back and forth if you want, pressing the board hard through the early part of each turn so you jump forward. The best place to learn pumping is on a slight downhill slope; you'll coast normally if you stand still, you'll slow down if you wedel in your turns, and you'll accelerate if you pump correctly. A second type of self-propulsion on the flatland, known as click-clacking or "the grapevine," requires the ability to do kick-turns in rapid succession. This method will be discussed under *"Wheelies and Kick-turns"* below.

Freestyle Tricks

1. WALKING THE BOARD

This trick is easiest to learn on a long, wide board. Push yourself along to a fast-walk or slow-run pace. Stand with both feet near the back of the board, and when you feel that your balance is good back there, take two quick little steps toward the nose of the board (see Illustration 33). The most precarious moment in the trick is when your legs are crossed; at the moment when your back foot is frontmost, you should make a little un-weighting motion with your arms and body so you don't have to balance all your weight on the crossed-over leg while you are uncrossing the other one and getting it up to the front where it belongs. As you get better at doing the walking trick, limit the unweighting motion to a mini-mum and make your feet move faster and faster until you can make it look like you are just flicking the board forward and back under you effortlessly. Although you can do more walking on a long board, many people think that the rapid-walking stunt looks most impressive on a board that's so small it doesn't look like the rider can stay on it.

2. HANGING TEN

This means hanging your ten toes over the nose end of the board as it coasts along. The trick follows walking naturally; you hustle on up to the nose of the board, then hang the ten toes over, then pull some kind of dramatic pose, like throwing your arms up over your head, or squatting down and putting your hands out in front of you, or throwing one arm out front and letting one trail along behind, or popping a nose wheelie (see page 101), or throwing your head back and howling. Whatever seems to fit your mood at the time.

3. SHOOT THE DUCK

This refers to what should be done if you throw your head back while hanging ten, and spot a mallard up in the air, zeroing in for a bombing run. No, it actually applies to a stance you can do after hanging ten. You balance on one foot just back from the nose of the board, then stick the other foot way out in front like a battering ram. Extending your arms out front along with the foot makes this trick look even more dramatic, and it helps your fore-and-aft balance. Pointing the extended toe looks neat too (see Illustration 55). Make sure you have good speed when shooting the duck, because it can get tricky trying to scramble up out of the shooting stance, and you'll need a little time.

4. POWER SLIDES

To do a power slide, you have to get up a great deal of speed, like a slow-run to fast-run pace, then you have to pick a place to pull the stunt off that will allow you to recover quickly and easily. For beginners, it's easiest to do power slides on a slope; you push along uphill until you are moving fast, then lean and turn sharply. You can turn either way, but most people go toward the side of their front foot to start with. As you go into the tight turn, lean way over and put the hand that's closest to the ground down on it, then swing your body and the board around that pivot hand. Push hard with your back foot, and the rear wheels will break loose and slide around, increasing the speed and sharpness of the turn. Note how Tony Carter is pushing the board with his back foot in Illustration 56. When the board has swung around so it is heading downhill, push off with your hand

illustration **55** Shooting the Duck

illustration **56** Power Slide

and stand up again. When you have learned how to master the power slide on a slope, try doing it back on the flat. It's harder work because you have to keep more momentum through the turn in order to get up out of it at the end, but it looks primo when it's done right. You can also do two-handed power slides, power slides to the opposite side from the one that comes natural to you, and four-wheel power slides, but these require more gymnastic twisting of the body, and they are easier to fall out of.

5. THE COFFIN

Lie down stiffly on your back while coasting along on the skateboard. Clasp your hands irreverently over your chest. Make an appropriate face. Wow, you're doing the coffin. It's hardly worth the effort of getting down there and struggling back up again, but it's different.

6. WHEELIES AND KICK-TURNS

To do the most simple wheelie, you plant your feet at opposite ends of the board (keep the front foot back a little from the nose), then lean back on your back foot until the front wheels come off the ground. This can be done when the board is coasting in a straight line, but it is much more often used as part of a kick-turn; as the front wheels start to come up off the ground you twist your body, so the front end of the board snaps smartly to the side toward which you twisted, then comes down, starting off again in a different direction. If the twisting motion of a kick-turn is increased, the turn can become a one-eighty (half a rotation while in the Wheelie) or a three-sixty. See Rotation Stunts, below. If the kick-turns are kept short and alternated, they can be used as a form of propulsion, called click-clacking or "the grape-vine." Pushing the board with your feet toward one side; then, before you lose your balance, do a quick kick-turn to get the nose back under you. Push to the other side, pull a second kick-turn, and so on. The rhythm and motion of the board is a little like the rhythm and motion of someone propelling themselves on ice or roller skates with those out-to-the-side kicks, but since you're doing

illustration **57** Kick Turn

it with only one skate under you, your body english and coordination have to be much better.

If you're into tightrope walking, you can do a very different sort of wheelie stunt, namely holding a wheelie for as long as possible, either while coasting downhill or while just standing still. These types of wheelies are often done while hanging ten on the nose of the board; the stunt gets more and more boring for the audience though, the better and better you get at it. A judge will give low marks for a five minute freestyle routine that consists of one motionless nose wheelie, no matter how impressive a feat of balance that is. There are other kinds of wheelies for variety in any routine, though, like heelies

illustration **58** Working up to a One-eighty

(with one or both feet at the back of the board), one foot wheelies (with only one foot on the board, and the other up in the air), and for gymnasts like champ Russ Howell, hand stand wheelies. One use of the wheelie that must be done with care is jumping down and climbing up curbs. If you do it right it looks neat, but if you slip, it's one of the quickest ways to destroy your skateboard or its trucks.

7. ROTATION STUNTS

This simply means extensions of the kick-turn into a circular motion, pivoting around the back wheels. The one-eighty is half a rotation. Three-sixties are full rotations. Although it is simple to say what a three-sixty is, doing it is no simple matter at all. The easiest way to learn is to practice riding with your back foot cocked around and hanging over the tail of the board like the guy has his in Illustration 58. When you feel comfortable doing that, try to lean your weight back on the foot until you do a wheelie, then do a kick-turn toward the side of your back foot (if you ride left foot back, turn to the left; right-foot-back riders, turn to the right). The farther you try to kick-turn in this manner, the more you will have to swing your arms and body to get the board around, and the longer you will have to hold the front wheels off the ground. To help you learn, you can do a big high wheelie so the back end of your board comes way down. Then you can drag the toe-end of your back shoe along the ground as a sort of pivot-brake, as in illus-

tration 58. A kicktail board, or a board with a Kevin
Reed tail-saver (see page 158) will give you something
to jamb your foot against so it doesn't get dragged off the
end of the board. When you can pivot about ninety
degrees or so by using this foot-dragging kick-turn, find
a place where there is a steep little incline that goes up
about ten feet or so, like up a driveway from the street,
and learn how to zip up the incline, do a kick-turn as
you slow, then coast back down the incline. When you've
mastered a full one-eighty on the incline, go back to
your flat practice area and start trying the three-sixty that
you've been building up to. It takes a big swing of the
arms and upper body; the rear wheels will tend to go
around in a small circle, rather than pivoting, especially
if you are using your back foot for a pivot against the
ground. Because of the tight-circling tendency, it's best
to do at least your first three-sixties at a low rate of
speed. When you have the trick pretty well wired, you can
stop using your back foot for a pivot, move your front
foot back to the middle of the board, and keep the nose
closer to the ground, so the back wheels can spin right
around each other without circling at all. Hold your
arms in close to your body during the spin, as Terry
Brown is doing in Illustration 59, and you'll spin faster
and longer.

Some of the many variations on the three-sixty that you
can work on after you have mastered the basic rotation
are: consecutive three-sixties (seven-twenties and so on,
which require a sort of board-bobbing, pumping action
in order to keep going), reverse three-sixties (turning in

illustration **59** Three-sixty

the opposite direction from normal, which is tough and treacherous if you fall), nose three-sixties (done standing on the nose instead of the tail), two-foot three-sixties (done with both feet at the same end of the board), head-dip three-sixties, and for the Russ Howell types, hand stand three-sixties. New variations that go over my head are cropping up all the time, as well as new ways to incorporate rotation stunts into other routines. The three-sixty is a flashy move, and almost always goes well as decoration for some other trick that may be difficult but isn't too spectacular. I think it's perfectly OK to do this sort of decoration. After all, everything you do on a skateboard can be seen as a form of ornament that you're setting down on all the ugly pavement around us. As Steinbeck says in *Sweet Thursday,* "when a man finally sees just how boxed-in he is, the first thing he does is to decorate the box." So go ahead, do that ornamental three-sixty whenever it fits in gracefully. The world needs it.

8. ENDOVER AND WALKOVER

Two tricks that use the techniques of the three-sixty but without calling for full rotations are the endover (or "endo") and the walkover. The endover is a continuous series of one-eighties, with the rider and board progressing more or less in a straight line as they spin. You have to practice this stunt a lot before you can learn to do the one-eighties in rapid succession, without any rolling inbetween. The trick makes a great sound, bop-bop-bopping along, and if you learn to do it with a minimum of arm flailing, and with a minimum of lift given to each end of the board during the time it is off the ground, it can look like an incredibly fluid ballet step. Wow; wouldn't that tall Russian ballet dancer named Maya Plisetskaya look great doing endos? I don't think the Kremlin would be too hot for it, though.

The walkover begins with a one-eighty in the direction toward your back foot side, and then goes to another one-eighty in the opposite direction, and so on. Some riders shorten each one-eighty more and more, until they are walking along with the board sideways, taking quick little bip-bip-bip-steps. The short steps are good for variety; but the walkover with full one-eighty steps is more dramatic if it is well-controlled.

9. TWO BOARD DAFFY

This trick gets its name from Daffy Duck, and is sometimes called the duck-walk. It is not too challenging, once you can get into the right position, and it is always good for a laugh or two. It involves riding along on the nose of one board as you coast toward a second waiting board, stepping onto the second board with your free foot, then putting both boards into wheelies. After a moment or two of balancing in that whacky pose (see Illustration 60), you can step onto the second board and coast away. The dangerous moment during the stunt is that moment when you have just stepped onto the second board, and you are popping two wheelies at once. Practice that critical step repeatedly, so if you have to do the daffy for competition or for an audience, you

illustration **60** Two Board Daffy

don't have to make three or four attempts to get into the
duck-footed stance. Foot placement is very important.
Also, make sure the boards are lined up straight, so they
don't go off in different directions.

10. HIGH JUMP

It's still an open question whether this stunt will be
recognized in free style competition, but even if it isn't,

it makes such a great show, and it's such an accomplishment, it's worth trying anyway. Wear knee and elbow pads and a helmet for SURE when learning the high jump.

Although the fine points of jumping are covered expertly by Bob Mohr in his article (Skateboarder, Vol. 2, No. 4), you can start to learn the basics by just riding along on a board and jumping off it a little as it rolls. That seems easy enough, especially on a long, wide, stiff board. But try jumping a little higher (you do have padding on, don't you?) and you'll discover that it's hard to jump in such a way that the board keeps going at the right speed and in the right direction so you can land on it without doing a horrible zzzzzip-SPLAT fall. It may seem wrong to you, but try to jump with the board going at a good clip, like a fast walk at least; that way it will have enough momentum when you are up off it to coast back under you. When you can jump pretty high, like two feet above the board, and land back on it without mishap every time, set up a jump bar as in Illustration 61. Start low. Concentrate on timing more than height, right from the start, and you'll do better as you go along. For one thing, the more times you do well-timed landings, the less time you will spend wearing casts. For another thing, the higher you try to jump, the more perfect your timing will have to be. So start right at the beginning by working hard on precision. Watch the board, not the bar. If, in the middle of a jump, you can see that you are going to hit the board at one end or out of balance, just spread your feet and land on the ground. It's almost impossible to make up for a bad jump when you hit the board cockeyed. Make sure you can do a one or two foot high jump perfectly and with plenty of extra height before you try the higher stuff. And for heavens' sake, whenever you try for more height, put the padding on if you have taken it off due to confidence at the lower elevations. On big jumps, the essential thing is to wait until the very last instant before lift-off, then convert *just* enough forward motion into vertical motion to get you over the bar *without* making the board stop down on the ground. It is especially important to land square and with your weight over the board when you come down from a high jump; you can try coming down one foot at a time to soften the landing, but if you can

illustration **61** High Jump

tell that you're coming down cockeyed, don't hesitate to spread the old feet and land on the ground. Practice, practice, and more practice at the lower levels will make your big jumps work at last. The real experts use medium-sized boards (26"–29") for their jumps, so when you have complete confidence jumping from a big board, you can try using the more difficult medium size; it makes the feat even more impressive, like diving off a fifty foot platform onto a damp sponge that's a *small* damp sponge.

11. AERIAL SPINNERS

Once you've learned to jump well, you can start taking on the Nuryev ballet stunt of spinning around in the middle of a jump. Spinners done while standing normally on the board are pretty simple and not too showy, but spinners up in the air are among the hardest and most impressive stunts. Try an aerial one-eighty spin first, just switching your feet front-to-back. Then, on a big, wide, stiff board, try a full three hundred and sixty degree spin. Whoooosh. That's a long way around, even if you just jump off the ground and do it. By the way, if you can tell at about three-quarters of the way around that you aren't going to make it, spread your feet and come down on the ground instead of the board. The spinning and cockeyed landing on a moving skateboard must be one of the best-designed landings for producing bone-breaking, muscle-stretching, brain-bashing falls. And it always *looks* so awful.

If you master the aerial spin and aren't willing to stop even there, you can try a helicopter, which involves jumping up and doing an aerial spinner while holding onto the board either with your toes (you have to do it barefoot), or with your hands. One ace rider can jump off the top of a table while crouching down and holding onto his board with his hands; he does a spinner before he hits the ground, then skates happily away. It's too much. Others tape their feet to the board, but this leaves you no escape route if you get into trouble in mid-air.

12. HAND STANDS AND HEAD STANDS

Hand stands are for the grandstands. Riding along on a skateboard on your hands is so difficult, so athletically demanding, and so limiting that I don't recommend it unless you are a devout gymnast and show-off. I am enough of a show-off that I'd like to do it, but I'm too skinny and too chicken. Learning to do the hand stand requires first learning to do stable hand stands on the

illustration **62** Hand Stand

flat ground, then doing a few while holding onto a short, narrow, *wheel-less,* and non-flexy skateboard that's sitting up on blocks or something. To do the trick on a regular skateboard, as it rolls along, you have to jump into the hand stand from the side, then balance by shifting your weight over your hands, and steer by tipping your hands from side to side. Ever notice how strong Ross Howell looks in the pictures? There's a simple reason.

Head stands, although they are not quite so physically demanding, are really even harder to perform than hand stands because you have to either stand backwards on the board and then go into a forward-facing head stand, or start facing forward and wind up in a head stand facing backwards. Do the stunt without a helmet if you want (your head is down on the ground anyway, so it can't fall far) but don't try it at any faster speed than a slow walk, and make sure the pavement is very smooth and pebble-free. It can be a jarring experience otherwise.

For the final step up to gymnastic freestyle excellence, you can try a no-hands head stand, or an L-sit into a hand stand. The first requires unbelievable balance, and I don't know of anybody who's done one that lasted more than a few feet. The L-sit into a hand stand has been done, however. You have to squat on the board, put your hands down on the ends of it, then raise your legs out in front of you and hold yourself up in the air in the sitting position. As if that isn't enough, you then swing and coil your legs under you and up until you can raise yourself into a frog stand, or a horizontal "flange" position. From the flange or the frog stand you lift your body and legs up to the vertical position by brute force, all the while keeping the board balanced. Yaaack! If you are up to it, I congratulate you. You can go on to insane things like jumping curbs in the hand stand position, doing hand stand three-sixties, hand stand endovers, and walking up all 438 steps to the top of the Washington Monument, ON YOUR HANDS ON A SKATEBOARD.

DO YOUR OWN TRICK

The above list of tricks is not all-inclusive. It isn't even a very broad sampling of the known tricks. If you want a better sampling, see Russell Wayne Howell's beautiful little photo book, "The Handbook of Freestyle Skateboard Tricks," (Cowboy Star Publications, 246 N. Fries Ave., Wilmington, California, 90744), or the more fully explained and diagramatic "Skateboarding," by Jack Grant (Celestial Arts, 231 Adrian Road, Milbrae, California, 94030). These books can give you some nice ideas and pointers on the subject. Remember, though, to work most on the things that *you* like doing. If you happen to like some whacky sort of stunt that nobody's ever seen before, DO IT! Don't let the neighborhood hot-shots tell you it's wrong because it isn't a recognized stunt. If it's good and you do it often enough, believe me people will learn to recognize it; they'll start saying "WOW, look, there's Joe Blow (or whatever your name happens to be), doing one of his Joe Blow double floob-

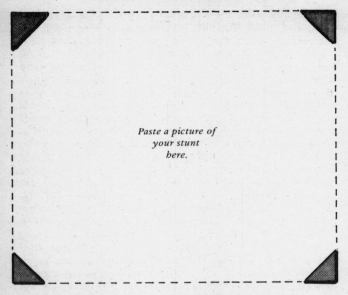

Paste a picture of
your stunt
here.

ers!" And maybe the Joe Blow double floober (or whatever you choose to call your stunt) will go down in the
annals of skateboarding as one of the truly great inno-
vations of flatland freestyle riding.

FREESTYLE EQUIPMENT

Different sorts of board tops are required for different
kinds of tricks. For tricks that require wheelies, three-
sixties, and hand stands, most riders like a small to
medium-sized board (24"–29" long, and 6"–7" wide)
that has a little flex but not too much. Many riders who
like doing their freestyle tricks barefooted or on their
bare hands like to have boards that don't get sharp
edges. Some like having a kicktail for wheelies and rotation stunts, but others do fine without kicktails. Some
polypropelene type board tops, especially the ones that
have a metal plate on the bottom, work fine for free-
styling. They're nice because they never chip, splinter, or
get sharp around the edges. Slightly heavier nylon-
fiberglass boards like those made of Du Pont Zytel, and

Lexan boards like the Roller Sports Pro are good for the same reason; they never get sharp around the rails. Many freestylers do use fiberglass or hardwood boards (great big wood boards flap around impressively when you do wheelies and rotation stunts) but they have to do occasional filing and sanding to keep from getting cut on their boards (see page 159). Aluminum boards are good if they are made from 190" thick 7075 or 2024 alloy with either T4, T6, or T8 treatment. These boards are costly, however, and the rails tend to get worn into knife-like edges. Cheap plywood boards are not recommended for freestyle tricks because they get so splintery. Acrylic boards like ones made of plexiglass or Lucite aren't too good either. They get weak and brittle in the sun and they chip around the rails.

For tricks that require more footroom (or headroom), like jumping, aerial spinners, and head stands, you'll want a longer board, like one that's 30 inches long or more. The wood ones like the Sims, the Brewer, the Logan earth ski, and the solid but awkward-looking Arrowsmith are all good for these stunts; you can make your own board top out of hardwood, but make sure the wood is either thick enough or of high enough quality to be good and strong. You don't want it to snap under you at an awkward moment in the middle of a stunt.

All freestyle boards, no matter what they're made out of, tend to wear down at the tail and at the nose. For some possible solutions to these nagging problems, see "Tail Dragging" on page 156.

Wheels for freestyle skateboards are often very different from those used for downhill riding. In all of the stunts other than the power slide, you want to have a wheel that will roll farther rather than one that will grip well and break into a slide smoothly. Freestylers get large diameter wheels for the most part, ones made from hard urethane, or ones with soft urethane on the outside and harder stuff near the core, like on the old-style Cadillac and Hang Ten wheels; these harder, larger diameter wheels require less pushing along or click-clacking to keep going, so more time is left for doing tricks. If you get big hard wheels for freestyle, just don't try wedeling down a steep hill on them. They go too fast and slide all over on steep hills.

Different trucks from the standard ones are also used on many freestyle boards. Because the flex and torque factors are not so great as they are in downhill riding, you can use steel trucks like the Chicago ones, or the Bahne-type stamped steel ones. Some riders like to get softer cushions for their trucks, like the Bennett red rubber cushions, or automobile shock absorber grommets like those described on page 119, while some like the quick, sensitive response of the whole Bennett truck. Other freestyle performers like the stiff feel of hard cushions, and the solid feel of the metal-to-metal contact of the pivot in its socket that you get with the Chicago or Bahne-type trucks. Those steel trucks *are* tight and positive when they are new, but they should not be used for so long that the pivots and pivot sockets get worn down and loose.

6

Radical Riding on Weird Terrain

OK, now we're getting to the more exotic side of skateboarding. Man has put concrete in all sorts of strange places to guard against heavy flows of water. River beds, drainage ditches, erosion-prone hillsides, and even underground streams have been covered with cement to keep the water from washing away soil or flooding nearby towns. Sometimes these great expanses of cement have caused more problems than they have solved because of their unnatural shapes. Over the years, engineers have learned that the smoother and the more naturally-curving they make their cement waterways, the better they work.

Smoothly rounded concrete is also used in swimming pools, not because of any consideration for natural water flow, but because the gently curving surfaces are easier to keep clean.

In some dry parts of the country, the bottoms of reservoirs have been cemented to hold the winter rains for summer irrigation. Because of the fact that these reservoirs are usually situated at the bottoms of steep ravines with curving sides, they often have banked walls.

All of the above water control or retaining devices are empty from time to time. The reservoirs dry up by late summer each year; many pools are empties for the winter months; drainage ditches are dry except during heavy rains; even the river and stream beds often dry up completely for several months of each year.

What a waste. All those nice paved surfaces just sitting around with nothing to do when they're dry. Here's what you can do to make sure your local expanses of cement don't go to waste: SKATE THEM!!! I won't be able to tell you how to ride the particular type of weird terrain where you live, but the suggestions made below will all be leaning toward riding aggressively; fast, hard, and with gusto. I call this radical riding. That doesn't mean fanatic left-wing type riding, it means riding that's "of or from the roots." That's how Webster defines radical. I'm talking about riding that gets to the fundamental questions of just how far you can push your skateboard and your ability in a situation that is extremely challenging. How sharp a turn can you make on a banked concrete wall? How fast can you ride through a jarring deflection without demolishing your board or losing control and falling? How fast can you power-slide at a 45 degree angle? How far can you ride up a vertical wall? Those are *radical* questions. They go to the roots of skateboarding.

A few words of caution before you set out with radical zeal to conquer every square inch of cement in sight. Don't climb fences with big NO TRESPASSING signs on them if you can possibly help it. And if you have to climb any fence at all to get to your chosen skateboarding haven, try to do it without damaging the fence, or some-

illustration **63**

body will come along sooner or later and make the fence higher. Don't leave any garbage around, either; if someone comes to say they don't like you skateboarding there, they'll just use your litter as an excuse to kick you out. After all, the skateboards themselves don't do any damage to the cement. It's the skateboard *riders* who people worry about. So if you find a nice place, keep it looking nice, and it won't get wired off or covered with "speed bumps" that make it impossible to skate on safely.

Whenever you want to try out a new-found spot for the first time, take a broom and a square-nosed shovel along to clean off any sand, gravel or dirt. Also, at all times, wear a helmet, gloves, and pads for your knees and elbows so you can feel free to explore the limits of your board and ability with a minimum of danger.

DRAINAGE DITCH RIDING

There are endless different shapes and sizes of storm drains that are good for skateboarding. They range from little parking lot gutters to gigantic spillways for dams. The sample shown in illustration 64 shows just a few of the many possible approaches to one sort of drain. The point on the left side of the ditch marked "Start" represents the highest point in the area, which is almost always the best place to begin any run through a ditch. The way to do the course that weaves back and forth across the ditch and disappears into the tunnel is to push off at the Start, coast down to the deflection and through it at an angle, bracing yourself for the jolt and unweighting by lifting your arms (see Illustration 65). Going across the bottom of the ditch, you might want to crouch to keep going fast, or you might do a quick pump or two if you're good at picking up speed that way; when you reach the deflection at the bottom of the right bank, you should still have enough speed to zoom up most of the way, then pull a nice smooth turn that doesn't slow you down, then maybe make one quick push with your foot or one pump for extra speed. The deflection will give you much bigger jolt this time, so be ready for it, unweighting with your hands up high (see Illustration 65). Angle across to the left side of the ditch at full speed.

illustration **64** Drainage Ditch Doodling

illustration **65** Hitting the Deflection

The angle of the deflection will be very sharp this time, so be prepared (if you didn't put padding and a helmet on like I told you to, you might pay for that error right *now*). When you have shot through the deflection and practically straight up that ridiculously steep left bank

illustration **66** One-eighty at the top—
Kevin Thornber

near the mouth of the tunnel there, you have to decide
quickly what to do. A smooth turn to the left will get
you over to less steepness, where you can come down
safely; if you're really going for it, though, you can pull
a quick one-eighty at the gravity-defying peak of your
last climb, as Kevin Thornber is doing in Illustration 66.
This will bring you down to your last deflection at a fast
clip, so once again, be ready. If you aren't going too fast
when you reach the bottom of the ditch, and there isn't
too much water or gravel down there, you can pull one
last sweeping, sliding turn and go howling off into the
tunnel, banking off its sides as high as possible, like
Scott Sommers is doing in the frontispiece photograph.

Once you have wired the climbing and descending
trip described above, you can try for an over-the-tunnel
shot, provided there is a cement lip up there to ride on.
The object is to get enough speed to go straight up the
steep portion of the right bank and over the mouth of
the tunnel, without getting up so much speed that you

wipe out at the bottom deflection before you start up the bank. Work up to the attempt by stages, doing one-eighties higher and higher up on the right bank, coming closer and closer to the top of the tunnel, and then finally taking a bit more speed and coasting over the top. You can come down at an angle after going over the tunnel, so you don't hit the descending deflection with too much speed. If anything goes wrong at the top of the tunnel, though, like if you lose speed or lose control or lose your nerve, make sure you fall toward the hillside, and fall quickly, before the skateboard slips sideways down into the tunnel and takes you with it.

If there is a ramp going down into a ditch, you can take a run at the edge of it, as shown, and do a little jump. Some people like doing really big jumps, with flips, twists, and full-gainers thrown in for the delight of onlookers, but I don't recommend these unless you have padding not only on yourself but on the ground where you will hit. If there isn't lots of padding, one of your dramatic twists might wind up being a permanent one. And if you have to skateboard around with a permanently twisted body, it won't look very dramatic.

When you can cover the basic courses like those above, or whatever courses come to you naturally in the ditch of your choice, you can start adding aggressive moves for the truly radical touch that seems to fit with riding in unusual terrain. Power slides in the turns, occasional three-sixties or even a five-forty at the top of a steep bank, nose-wheelies along tilting walls; things like that. You will begin to find the limits. Sometimes the limits will find you. Hopefully you will be padded, helmeted, and ready to roll loose when that happens.

RESERVOIR RIDING

There are many different sizes and shapes of reservoirs, and many don't have smooth concrete surfaces on which to skate. But among those that are nicely cemented over, most have sweeping curved surfaces, without particularly steep banks.

The gentler shape of most reservoirs naturally calls for a more sweeping, fluid style of riding, as can be done on

Reservoir Slalom
illustration 67

big wood boards. This doesn't mean that you can't work
hard and do lots of sliding, quick turning, nose-wheelie
riding, and kick-turning; it's just that the terrain doesn't
lend itself to the fast-action stuff. If the reservoir is built
on a grade, one fun thing you can do is start at the top,
push once or twice, then coast down one side to the
bottom of the bowl at high speed and crank a big hard
turn at the lower corner where it is banked. You can
work your way along the deflection, too, doing a whole
bunch of quick turns with little slides. Or you can set up
a slalom that uses the shape of the reservoir for variety,
as in Illustration 67. If there's water in the bottom of the
reservoir, and you have sealed bearing wheels, you can
always do a big arc up the bank nearest to the water and
end up with a graceful swan dive, but even if the water is
deep enough to permit this, it is often stagnant and
slimy; it doesn't make for a refreshing dip, but it is
radically different.

POOLS

Empty swimming pools are the skateboarder's dream. Many of them, especially the smaller oval and kidney-shaped ones, seem to have been designed specifically to challenge the utmost ability and courage of the skateboarder. Save pools for the last, for when you can be sure of your ability and your board in all kinds of situations. To really *do* a pool you've got to be able to call on a whole lot of skating experience; it'll take everything you know and then some.

Look for an empty pool that is clean, short (less than 30 feet in length), steep-bottomed (like one that drops from 4 feet to 10 feet deep in a short distance along the bottom), and either round, oval, or kidney-shaped (see Illustration 68). Depending on whether you live in Southern California or Northern Maine, finding such a pool may be pretty easy or extremely hard. Once you've found the best local pool, it's a good idea to keep quiet about it. Not just because it's hard to skateboard in a crowded pool, but also because the more people there are using a pool, the sooner somebody will get hurt, and the sooner the pool's owners will get worried about the risk and fill the pool up again or chase everyone out and lock the place up.

Prepare your chosen pool for use by sweeping out all sand, gravel, dust, and dried-up scum along the sides and

illustration **68**

illustration **69** Over the Taped Light

bottom. This takes some hard work sometimes, but it makes for less spin-outs and crashes. Make sure the surfaces are all dry, too, so nobody will get their wheels wet and then slide out of control halfway up a vertical wall. Cover the pool drain with something like a cushion or a piece of sponge rubber, then either remove the glass cover for the pool light, or tape it over with thick, strong cloth tape like the grey gaffer's tape that movie cameramen use; this will probably save it from breaking, and even if it does crack or come loose, the tape will keep it from shattering and cutting you (see Illustration 69).

The way to learn how to ride a pool is to start at the bottom and work your way up, wearing a helmet, gloves, and elbow pads at all times. To get just a bit of a feel for the curve at the deep end of a pool, start a few feet up the incline and toward one side, then coast down near to the side and bank around the deep end curve a foot or so up from the bottom. Right away you'll notice that you tend to be pushed by the centrifugal force in such a way that you fall forward against the wall. After a couple of falls like that, you'll start leaning more toward the center of the pool as you go through the curve; when you do this, your feet go much faster around the curve than your head does. It's an odd sensation, but you can get used to it if you just concentrate on making your feet do the turn while you keep the rest of your body perpendicular to the

board. *Don't* twist your body and try to keep straight up
in relation to the rest of the world; this is the natural
tendency, but it doesn't work with all that centrifugal
force. Watch somebody else as they glide through a turn
on the lower bank of the pool, and you'll see that their
bodies are sticking out perpendicular to the board,
whether the board is horizontal, at an angle, or vertical
up on the wall. Notice how both Tony Carter and Tim
Piumarta are perpendicular to their boards in Illustration
68, even though their boards are at different angles on
the wall of the pool. Tim (top) has to be horizontal
because his board is vertical. Tony is sticking up at an
angle because his board is only tipped about half-way as
it goes through the banked lower part of the curve.

When you have wired the low-level turns, letting your
feet do the turning so the rest of you can handle the
centrifugal force, you can try to stretch the high point of
your turn higher and higher up the wall. To do this, you
have to start higher up the incline for speed, and you
have to make your turn up on the wall sharper and
sharper. This means that you hit the deflections going up

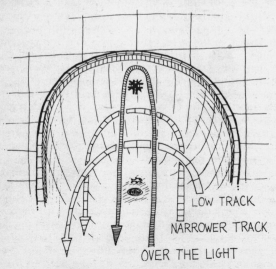

LOW TRACK

NARROWER TRACK

OVER THE LIGHT

illustration 70 Pool Tracks

illustration **71** Tim Hits the Tile

and down at sharper and sharper angles, so you have to brace for them, before and after doing the quick turn up on the wall. It's a lot to do in a short period of time. But after a few falls and quick runs out of cross-ups, you'll be going straight down one side of the incline, passing the drain, shooting up the wall, banking and turning hard, then shooting back down and past the drain, making a narrower track than when you were just learning.

The last big step is the attempt to go over the pool light and get up to the coveted blue tile, the source of "blue tile fever." In all except the shallowest of pools, getting over the light is so difficult that it requires a different approach from the normal banking and curving at lower elevations. You have to get going up the wall at optimum speed and in just the right "track" to get as near as possible to the top of the light. As you begin to lose momentum and go into the weightless moment at the top of your ascent, do a little "kip" with your knees to get the board actually above your body and over the light. Illustration 71 shows Tim Piumarta doing the kip up onto the blue tile. Whoosh. It's hard, let me tell you. I can't come close. And you do a lot of running down

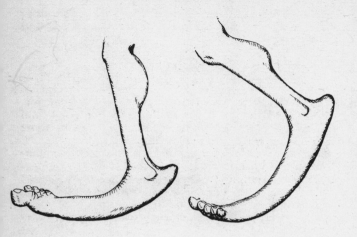

illustration **72** Pool Feet

the wall trying to learn. In fact, one problem is that your natural urge, at that last weightless moment when you should be doing a kip like a champion gymnast, is to bail out and run down as fast as you can. But even bailing out and running is tough, because your feet smack down terrifically hard as they try to fight the centrifugal force *and* the gravity getting you back to the bottom of the pool. Because of this fierce foot-smacking running (a doctor told me it's probably putting something like 25 to 30 thousand pounds of force per square inch on your feet) it is much better to do all pool riding with good sturdy rubber-soled shoes on. People who try it barefoot wind up with bizarre and painful foot injuries.

For those who finally master the consummate art of riding the blue tile or even touching the lip at the top of the tile, there isn't much left to do in life. You can try passing another skater going the opposite direction, as in Illustration 67, or do an upside-down power-slide over the light, or see how far along the blue tile you can extend the weightless top of your curved track, or you can try to jump all the way *out* of the pool, but your radical riding will have reached a sort of zenith, after which everything may seem a little tame, until you find a deeper pool.*

RADICAL RIDING EQUIPMENT

Whatever you choose to ride on for your radical attacks on weird terrain, it better be strong and reliable. It will take a beating if you really go for the limits, and if it isn't durable it will fall apart, break, or in some other way fail when you don't want it to.

One proven combination of parts is a stiff, medium-sized (6" to 9" longer than your stance length, as measured in Illustration 1) pultruded fiberglass board, raised up fairly high over wide, high-quality trucks with large, long-lasting wheels; a beefy outfit.

Since you'll probably want large wheels for durability and easy rolling on rough surfaces, you should try to get either high-built trucks or wide ones that adapt well to being put up on risers. The Bennett truck is very good in design, but it might seem over-sensitive in its handling, and it tends to break if you are heavy or overly rough on it. The Brewer truck, which costs less, has a more standard steering response. With big wheels, the normally vulnerable main bolt head won't hit the ground, and everything else about the Brewer truck is strong and beautifully crafted by a master machinist. If you want a board with a wide wheelbase, one that won't be affected too much by being lifted up over big wheels on risers, get Tracker trucks. They will put up with incredible punishment, and give you a sure-footed ride. The heavier steel

---

* A couple of new radical riding techniques are being used. One consists of riding from side to side of the curved walls of big (18 foot diameter) drain pipes or swimming pools. If you pump on each descent while doing this, just as if you were on a swing, you'll find that you can make your skateboard into a hair-raising perpetual motion machine, going higher and higher after each pump. Another option for you radical riders who don't live around any good weird terrain is to make your own banks and bowls out of big 4 x 8 sheets of plywood. Just make sure the frame holding the plywood is sturdy, and make all the joints between the sheets smooth. To avoid splinters and to improve traction, you can paint over the plywood with liquid urethane. On warm days, the stuff will get soft and provide super grip for urethane wheels.

Continental trucks are almost as strong, but not as wide; they aren't as responsive with their hard stock cushions, either.

If you need risers for any of the trucks mentioned, you can use 9-ply birch plywood or neoprene rubber to absorb some of the shocks encountered when skating over rough surfaces. Don't use soft rubber risers that are over a quarter inch thick, though, or they'll squish out of shape and get loose. You can cut risers out of the sidewall of a tire with a sharp knife if you want to have rubber ones that won't allow the trucks to work loose.

With your tough board held up on big trucks or high risers, you can have large diameter, fast-rolling wheels like the Roller Sports Big Wheels, or the big Road Riders, both of which have been proven over a long period of time, or you can try one of the newer wheel types like the Sims giant wheels, or the Flex-edged Power Paws or Bennett Alligators, or the thick, smooth-rolling Rolls Royce Silver Cloud wheels. They all have their good points, and good riders with different tastes will swear by all of them. Try to get a wheel that has a reputation for durability, though; ask around about any wheel you are considering and see if it can put up with rough treatment for as long as the standard-setting Road Rider.

If you can't afford to step up to big wheels and trucks, and are forced to use your standard-sized equipment on a fiberglass board, you will experience a very rough ride on uneven surfaces. The vibrations go right through the small wheels and the trucks, then travel along the surface of the fiberglass until they get to your feet. Many tough young riders aren't bothered by these vibrations, and they would feel short-changed if they weren't right in touch with them. Other riders, especially old coots like me, find all that ratta-tatta-tatta a little too painful after awhile. We are forced to get one of the alternatives below, either hard-to-find strong wood boards, or expensive aluminum ones, or non-resilient boards, or cheap wood boards that work, but aren't made to last forever. If we don't get the good old fiberglass, in other words, we have to give up something, but it can be worthwhile in the long run.

Whatever the board is made from, it should be stiff enough that when you stand in the middle of it, it only bends about a half inch. If you get a more flexible board, like most of the archery bow laminated ones, you'll find that you have to stand with your feet over the trucks to keep the board steady in rough, deflecting terrain. What you want is a board that's stiff enough so you can control *its* reactions, rather than *its* flexy twang controlling *you*. If you have gotten good at controlling the twang of a Fibreflex type board, OK, but for me, a stiffer board seems to make more sense.

Super-strong hardwood boards are about the best choice next to fiberglass, but they are hard to find. You'll have to look around your area and see what's available, but for some examples, there's Sims in Santa Barbara, Logan Earth Ski in Encinitas, Brewer in San Clemente and Haleiwa, Hawaii, Kevin Reed (who makes a tough new laminated oak and fiberglass board) in Santa Cruz, Fox of West Palm Beach, Florida, and Arrowsmith of Austin, Texas. Well-made hardwood boards can put up with almost anything you can dish out. Some are even made with a little twang, so they smooth out the roughness of weird terrain.

If you can't find a top quality wood board maker in your area, but you don't want a harsh fiberglass board, you have three choices: use a sturdy plastic board, blow a bunch of money on a high-grade aluminum board, or make your own funky pine board that can be replaced when it gets saggy or worn out.

Among the many plastic boards, the best polypropelene ones seem to hold up pretty well under rough usage, although they don't have much twang. The Lexan board tops, like the Pro Line of Roller Sports, are plenty strong, and they're most resilient. Both the Lexan and the polypropelene boards have the nice quality of being able to flex in any direction; they will torque and twist in angular deflections and come back to shape immediately, whereas the unidirectional fiberglass boards resist twisting. The only trouble with almost all of the plastic boards is their small size.

High grade aluminum alloy boards can be made strong enough for radical riding. If you get a board that is .190" thick, and made of very high strength aluminum that has been treated to increase its stiffness, such as either 7075 or 2024, treated T4, T6, or T8, or a magnesium-aluminum alloy, it will last well, and dampen the shocks coming up from the pavement, too. But it will be very expensive in comparison to the standard fiberglass board top, and it'll be hard to find a dealer who knows for sure if any of the aluminum boards he has are up to those demanding specifications. If you do get an aluminum board and have trouble with the edges getting worn down until they are sharp, see page 157.

For those of you who want to make a strong radical riding board for yourself, you can either get a piece of very special, high-grade hardwood, or you can go to the other extreme and make a cheap pine board that won't last forever, but will be easy to replace as often as is needed.

To make a hardwood and birch-ply board that will last almost forever, get some air-dried, 3/8" thick (or 1/2" thick for a board longer than 36 inches) hickory, lemonwood (degame) or purple heart (amaranth). Make sure the piece you get is straight-grained and free of cracks or warping. It's hard to find these woods anymore, because they aren't used for archery bows as much as they used to be, but you can try at your local hardwood supply houses and lumber yards. If all else fails, write to The Craftsman, 2525 Mary Street, Chicago, Illinois, and they'll send you a catalogue that has many exotic hardwoods to choose from. Follow the instructions for the slalom board on page 84, and you'll wind up with a board that'll take almost anything you can dish out.

The great economy board for radical riding on weird terrain is the homemade pine special. It is far and away the cheapest board you can get, it's easy to make, and it will last surprisingly long if you make it carefully.

Go to the lumber yard and pick out a piece of 3/4" by 8" kiln-dried pine, of the length that you need for your board. Hunt around and find a piece with the grain running the right way, as in Illustration 73. You want the narrow grain-lines to run along the width of the board, not along the rail as in Illustration 6. This will keep the board from breaking in half. Do *not* get a piece of pine with any large knots or big wavy sections of grain that indicate there was a knot just to one side of the board. Pine is very weak around the knots, but relatively strong where the grain runs straight. You can plane down your

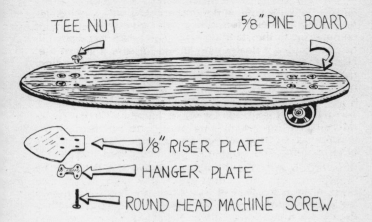

illustration **73** Pine Board

piece of clear dry pine if you want to make a skateboard with a little flex to it; for light riders (under 125 pounds) who want a shorter board (24″ to 27″), the pine can be planed down to ½″ thickness. For medium size and weight riders, ⅝″ will do. For heavy guys (over 175 pounds) or people who want a long board (over 32″), leave the pine at its full ¾″ thickness. Planing down even a pine board can be tedious and boring, so if you can get access to a wood shop at school or at a boys' club or through a friend's father, machine-plane the piece down to the thickness you want. When the piece is the thickness you want, check its flex and strength by the test-block method described on page 7 to make sure it isn't too thick or too thin for you.

You can pick a pattern from the ones on page 11 or copy a friend's by turning his board upside down on yours and tracing around it. Use a shape that's fairly wide, (6 inches at least) so you have enough footroom. Cut out the pine board with a coping saw, a saber saw, a band saw, or a jig saw. Then buy ⅛″ or ¼″ 5-ply birch (get it at a hobby shop), ⅛″ plywood if you plan to ride on small wheels, or ¼″ plywood if you have big wheels like those mentioned above. Cut the riser plates into the shape shown in Illustration 73, so they will leave clearance for the wheels when you lean into a sharp turn. If you are going all the way and using big wheels *and* wide trucks like the Trackers, you'll have to use not only ¼" riser plates but also risers at least ⅛" thick on top of the riser plates. These additional risers only need to be as big as the bottoms of the truck hangers. Once you have picked out and cut the riser plates and risers you need, get number 8 machine screws (or number 12, for Trackers) that are not quite long enough to go through the hanger plates, the risers and/or riser plates, and the board. Be precise about the length of these screws; if they're too long they'll stick up above the deck of the board; they're short they won't stay tight in the Tee nuts. Place the riser plates and risers so they are centered on the board (draw a center line on the board, as in Illustration 18, to get them right) and clamp them there with C-clamps. Then draw a center line on the risers and make hanger placement lines. Put the hanger plates where you want them, and drill the 5/32" guide holes for your number 8 machine screws (drill 3/16" guide holes for the big Tracker screws). Run the bit in and out of each hole a few times so the screws will slide in easily. Then unclamp the C-clamps, turn the board over, and drill wider holes down from the deck of the board for the Tee nuts. Used a 13/64" bit to drill the hole for the number 8 Tee nut (use a 15/64" bit for the Tracker size), and wrap some tape around the drill bit ¼" up from the end so you don't drill the hole too deep into that soft pine (see Illustration 21 to get the idea). Pound the Tee nuts into the top of the board, giving each one a couple extra whacks to make it sink down into the wood so it is flush with the deck.

Put a drop or two of the red Loctite "Stud and Bearing Mount" resin (you should be able to borrow a little of this from a neighborhood automotive mechanic) on the threads of each machine screw. Smear a strong glue like Elmer's or Titebond aliphatic resin on the riser plates, set the hanger plates in place, and screw the machine screws into the Tee nuts. Cinch them down well, putting the board on a table so you can press hard on the screwdriver as you tighten each screw. Check around the edges of the riser plates. If the edges aren't all squeezed down against the pine, clamp them with C-clamps, then leave the board overnight so the glue can set well.

Next morning, before you mount the trucks on the hanger plates, round off the rails of your board by planing, filing, and sanding them smooth. Then get some non-slip grip tape (or deck tape, as the boaters call it) and put it on the top of the board as in the patterns on page 41. Your pine board will get dangerously slick unless you take this precaution. Finally, to keep the board from getting beat up too quickly, and to prevent warping, rub some linseed oil into it with a rag and let it dry in the sun for a couple hours. If you apply linseed oil like that once every couple weeks or so, it will keep the board from getting dry, splintery, and weak.

Your pine board will be very usable and light, although not as thin and not quite as responsive as the fiberglass boards. The best thing about a pine board, though, is that it doesn't take too much money and time to make, so you can use it roughly while doing all kinds of radical attacks on rough terrain.

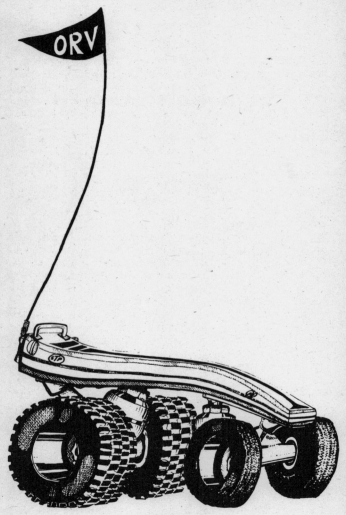

illustration 74

7

Transportation on a Skateboard

For the most part, getting from place to place on a skateboard is still a dream. Streets and roads were not made with skateboarders in mind. To get around in a town, you have to either keep jumping up and down curbs and watching out for cars in the intersections, or you have to ride out in the street and watch for cars *all* the time. Don't mix with cars if you can avoid them; you'll always come out on the short end. It's hardly worth the trouble to commute on your skateboard unless you live within walking distance of your school or your job, and can enjoy sidewalk riding between the dangerous street crossings. In many towns, riding skateboards in the street it prohibited anyway.

In the country, the roads often have rough surfaces that make it hard to keep up momentum on a skateboard. If, however, you live at the top of a big hill and go down it every day, and if the road is smoothly paved, and if there isn't any traffic coming up the hill, you might be able to do a one-way commute on the skateboard and hitch a ride back home on some other form of transportation.

The best thing about a skateboard is that when you find it too tiresome or uncomfortable, all you have to do is pick it up and hitch a ride on some other form of transportation. You can attach your skateboard to a bike frame, as shown in Illustration 43, or you can turn it

135

upside down and sit on it on a motorcycle, or you can carry it with you in a car, a bus, a train, a subway, or an airplane. And wherever you arrive, you can almost bet there'll be some pavement around to ride on. In fact, some wild riders are even taking their skateboards with sealed bearing wheels out into the woods to try them on steep trails. Who knows? The day may come when skateboards like the one in Rick's drawing (Illustration 74) are common. Uphill travel might be a problem, though.

If you want to get into long-distance traveling on roads, think twice. I mean, if you're going to wind up hitch-hiking maybe you'd be better off just tucking the board under your arm and hitching from the start. If you're dead set on breaking the long-distance record for your area or something like that, try to keep your luggage to an absolute minimum, so you won't have stuff flopping all around you like the guy in Illustration 75. Carry the few things you need like water and a little food and tools in a small, tight-fitting pack that won't bounce up and down as you push along; the kind that fits around your middle like a big belt is perfect.

For commuting or long distance travel on a skateboard, equipment must be carefully selected. You want a light, medium-sized board (about six to nine inches longer than your stance length as in Illustration 2), made of shock-absorbing material, like polypropelene, Lexan, aluminum, or wood and fiberglass lamination. The board should be fairly stiff, though, or you will waste energy bobbing up and down on it as you push along. Any strong truck will work all right, unless you want to do a lot of sharp turning as you descend hills, which will require a high truck or a regular truck on risers. Wide trucks are nice and stable, but they seem harder to keep going, so you may want to avoid them. You should try to get soft cushions, like the Bennett Red rubbers (see page 143) not only for their shock-absorbing properties, but because you can tighten the main bolt down on them and thus avoid the wobbles at high speeds as you coast down long straight hills.

As for wheels, to my way of thinking there is only one choice; the large Road Riders. These roll easily, last extremely long, and have fairly good traction if you need to turn sharp for some reason. Most other large wheels, like the Roller Sports Stokers or the big Sims wheels or the big Power Paws are all wide or shaped to thin shoulders for traction; this makes them have more rolling resistance, which is a pain in any long-distance ride. There are some large hard-core wheels, like the older ones made by Cadillac, that are fast on smooth downhill stretches, but the hardness makes these wheels ride rough, using up energy and slowing you down on level terrain. If you have to use open-bearing wheels for long-distance riding or commuting, you *must* clean and adjust them regularly, as described on page 139. Dirty loose wheel bearings create lots of friction.

illustration 75

8

Repairs
and Adjustments

Just because a skateboard is a relatively simple piece of machinery doesn't mean it is trouble-free. The truth is, when something goes wrong with a skateboard, it usually goes wrong in a big way, making the board unstable or dangerous. The trick is to take care of your skateboard and avoid the troubles. Keep an eye on all of the parts and watch out for the beginnings of little problems before they turn into big dangerous problems. If, for instance, you hear a cracking noise when you weight and unweight the board, find out what's causing it! It might be that the board is about to break, or that one of the truck hangers is about to snap in two. If you see crack lines running down the middle of the board or running across the board near one of the trucks, REPLACE THE BOARD!!! Right now, before it snaps and plunks you down on the pavement. If you hear rattly noises coming from one of your trucks, find out what is loose and tighten it up before it falls apart. If the wheels are making crackly loose noises, or grindy dirty bearing noises, take them apart, clean them, put them back together, and *adjust* them properly, before they self-destruct. If a wheel gives any hint of coming apart, like if the bearing cups start working loose in the urethane, REPLACE THE WHEELS before one fails all of a sudden and stops underneath you. Keep your eyes and ears open, that's the idea. Watch for the problems listed below, and

138

take care of their solutions before you take a bad fall due to equipment failure.

CRACKLY-GRINDY WHEELS

Your wheel bearings make weird and unnatural gritty or squeaky noises when you ride your board. If you have open bearings, it's time to overhaul them and adjust them, especially if they are loose or tight (frozen). Do the procedure described in the paragraphs below. If you have shielded "precision" bearings, the kind that aren't adjustable, you can try blowing the grit out with an air hose at a gas station, but you'll probably have to change the wheels, as in "Wheels Shot," below. If you have sealed precision bearings, and they are squeaky or gritty sounding, skip down five paragraphs and read how to do your greasing.

Begin the open bearing overhaul by using a socket tool (as in Illustration 15) to loosen (counter-clockwise) and remove the axle nut. Jiggle and pull the "D" washer off the end of the axle; use a pair of needlenose pliers to grip it and pull it off if you need to. Then hold the wheel over a nice clean rag that you have shaped into a bowl so it will catch all the ball bearings. Spin the outer cone off (counter-clockwise) with your fingers if they'll fit in there, or use the wide socket of your socket tool. Make sure all of the little ball bearings shower down into the nice bowl you made in the rag. When the cone is all the way off, take the wheel off too. You can leave the inner cone on the axle, but tighten it (clockwise) firmly; loose inner cones often cause wheels to freeze up on the bearings. Get a strong cleaning solvent, put some on a clean cloth, and wipe off the cones, the bearing cups inside the wheels, and the ball bearings themselves. If you are using a petroleum-based solvent and you have a Lexan board, make sure none of the solvent gets on the board top; it will attack the plastic and make it all lumpy and soft.

When the ball bearings and the bearing surfaces are clean, take a close look at them. Are they pitted or worn? The ball bearings will be a dull grey color if they are worn, rather than shiny. Each of the surfaces of the cones and the cups will have a shiny ring worn in it where the balls were running around and around, and if this ring is irregular in width or marked by tiny little pits that appear in patches, it is an indication that the cone or the wheel must be replaced. The cones usually wear out before the cups in the wheels, which is lucky because they are much easier to replace. When you go to your local skateboard supplier to get new parts, make sure you get a few extra 3/16" ball bearings in case you lose some, and if you get cones, make sure they fit your axle. Check the axle for bends or stripped threads; if it needs replacement, you might as well do it now while you have the wheels off (see "Axle Bent," below). Also, see if you can get self-locking aero stop nuts (the kind with the nylon ring in the threads) to use as axle nuts; they never jiggle loose like regular axle nuts do.

With your new or clean and shiny wheel parts all collected, put the wheel over the end of the axle with the inner side (the side that's flat and has a shallow hole down to the bearing cup) toward the truck. Screw the outer cone onto the axle a few turns (clockwise), then tip the board up so you can dribble the eight inner ball bearings into the wheel (see Illustration 23 on page 35 for how to do it). Hold the wheel against those inner bearings so none of them can sneak out and run away, then turn the board over so the outside of the wheel is up. Dribble the eight outer ball bearings into place, then screw the cone down onto them. If the outer balls all cluster in a tight ring around the axle and refuse to be pushed up into their proper place by the cone, just tip the board over again and they will fall into place (you did have the cone screwed in as far as possible, I hope, because if you didn't all them squirrely little balls may come scampering out).

Adjusting open bearings: When the ball bearings have been coaxed into their proper positions, turn the outer cone in (clockwise) until it is snug against the bearings, making the wheel a little hard to turn. Slide the "D" washer onto the axle, then turn the axle nut on (clockwise) with your fingers or a socket tool until it stops against the washer. Now fit the large socket of the tool over the outer cone, and turn the cone *counter-clockwise*

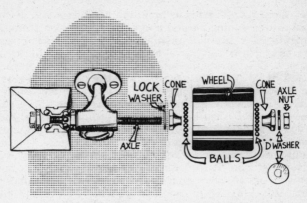

illustration **76** Open Bearing Wheels

until it is locked firmly against the "D" washer and the
axle nut. This last turn loosens up the bearings just the
right amount in most cases, and locks the cone and axle
nut at the same time, so they won't come loose. Do the
last counter-clockwise turn of the cone *firmly*. Not so
hard that you strip all the axle threads, but hard enough
so you're sure it won't come loose. Spin the wheel. It
should spin freely on the bearings, but it shouldn't have
more than a tiny bit of play if you try to move it from
side to side. If the bearings are too tight, loosen the axle
nut about a quarter turn and tighten (counter-clockwise,
remember) the cone up against it again. If the bearings
are just a little loose, you can usually turn the axle nut
clockwise a smidgen and correct the problem. Don't
crank too hard on that axle nut, though, or you'll strip
the weak threads on the end of the axle.

Give your cleaned and adjusted wheel bearings a treat
when you are done with them; buy a little Super Skate
Spray or some graphite lubricant like dri-slide, and puff
a bit into the works from both sides of each wheel. Then
when you go for your first ride it'll be smooth and quiet,
as well as clean and properly adjusted.

To lubricate sealed precision bearings, unscrew (counter-
clockwise) the axle nut of the squeaky wheel, then slide

the wheel off. If both bearings stay in the wheel, get a round stick or the eraser end of a pencil and push it through one bearing at an angle so it can poke the other one out. When you have both bearings out, check to see if they are double-sealed or single-sealed. Single-sealed bearings can be greased from the non-sealed side. Put lightweight grease like lithium-base automobile distributor cam lubricant, or high-quality waterproof bicycle grease all over the bearings; shove it in there around the lumpy metal retainer with a clean pencil tip or something so the ball bearings get a good dose.

Before you can grease double-sealed bearings, you have to take off one of the seals; poke a pin under the tiny ring of soft sealing material that fits against the inner metal sleeve of the bearing and pop the whole seal out of place. Now you can apply grease as described above for the single-sealed bearing.

When reconstructing the wheel (see Illustration 22) put the washer, the adapting shim (if you have one for a small axle), the inside bearing and the spacer on first, then push the wheel onto the inside bearing. Press the outer bearing into place, then tighten the axle nut down (clockwise). Make sure the unsealed sides of your greased bearings are on the inside of the wheel, so the grease will stay in there.

WOBBLY WHEELS *(loose trucks)*

This problem usually appears when you are going fast. By the time you are aware of it, the "speed wobs" have thrown you out of control and off your board. When you recover, you'll want to either fix those damn wobbly wheels or give up skateboards altogether. Before you do anything drastic, check for a few simple possible causes of the problem. Is the lock nut on the main bolt loose? Tighten it if it is. Are the wheels loose on the bearings? Adjust them as on page 140 if they need adjustment. Are the screws that hold the trucks to the board loose? Tighten them firmly if they are. Any of these simple problems could have caused your speed wobs, but more than likely the cause was that the main bolt was too loose. And the main bolt was probably loose because you loosened it so you could turn more easily (see page 49).

And you had to loosen it too much because the cushions were too hard. THIS is the real root of your problem: hard cushions. So right now, while you're still aching from your fall, you should go to the trouble of replacing the hard cushions with softer ones.

Cushion Replacement: Any time you need new or softer cushions, you should try to get the Bennett Red Rubbers. If they aren't available at stores where you live, you can order a set from Mr. Bennett, P.O. Box 1415-S, Newport Beach, Calif., 92663. Send two dollars for a set of four, plus twenty cents for postage. There are two different sizes; the large one goes nearest to the hanger plate, and the small one goes nearest to the head of the main bolt. If you can't get ahold of the Bennett cushions, try to find soft ones like those used in the California slalom trucks, the X-caliber trucks, or the Brewer trucks, or the super-soft grey ones that are used in Trucker trucks. If you can't find any of those, try to find soft urethane cushions. Most are too hard, but you can soften these by popping any bubbles you find in them with a pin, then sticking them in boiling water for fifteen to twenty minutes. Don't leave them in any longer or they will begin to break down. If you can't come up with any stock cushions that are softer than the ones on your trucks, go to a big car parts store and get four shock absorber grommets, the type that look like skateboard cushions. That's what the "Skateboard King" Bob Moore did for years when he couldn't find better cushions. ANYTHING is better than the hard rubber cushions that come in most standard trucks like the Sure Grip and Chicago ones. If you want some idea of how hard a prospective cushion is in relation to your standard one, just bite it between your front teeth and see how hard it is to squish the "O" shape of the center hole into a wide oval shape. A hard cushion will be almost impossible to squish. Your teeth will dent into a nice soft cushion and squish it easily.

When you have picked up four soft cushions compare their size with the size of the original cushions. If they are a little small in diameter or a bit tall, don't worry about it; they'll squish out when you cinch the main bolt down on them. If they are much too large in diameter, however, don't use them; the cushion caps will cut into them and they will get frayed and sloppy. If they are the right diameter but much too thick, put them in a vice and cut through them with a razor knife or a hacksaw. If they are thinner than your old cushions, or much softer so that when you squeeze down on them they wind up thinner, you have to do a little adjusting of the main bolt position. If you don't, the main bolt will pull down too far, altering the steering geometry and making it less responsive than it should be. Get a few thick washers that fit around the main bolt (rubber faucet washers are good) and save them to do the necessary adjusting after you have changed the cushions.

To change the cushions, first loosen (counter-clockwise) the lock nut on the main bolt a half turn or so, then hold it with your fingers as you unscrew (counter-clockwise) the main bolt with your skate key or a screwdriver. Take the main bolt out by pulling it to the side when it is unscrewed, then take the truck pivot out of its socket in the hanger plate. Now you can spin the lock nut off the end of the main bolt and pull the metal cushion caps, the rubber or urethane cushions, and the yoke of the truck off the main bolt. If your new cushions are soft and squishy like they should be, you will now need to file off the little metal tab or "dog" that is under the head of the main bolt (see Illustration 77). This little tab sticks into the dents in the cushion cap, and if you leave it in place, it will try to make the cap and the soft new cushion spin around as you tighten the bolt. The cushion will get all skewered out of shape and shredded, and will wear out quickly. If you file the tab off the main bolt, the bolt will spin and the cap and cushion will stay still, so you can get the whole business snug enough to keep you from ever getting speed wobs again.

When you have your custom-filed main bolt ready, slip the first cushion cap around it, then push the first soft cushion into place. Put the bolt through the truck yoke, then push the second cushion and the other cap into place, all in order as shown in Illustration 77. But before you spin the lock nut onto the main bolt, put on washers if you need them to make up for either thin or super-soft cushions that will alter the truck's turning geometry.

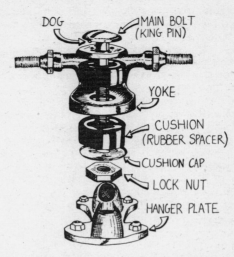

DOG   MAIN BOLT
             (KING PIN)

YOKE

CUSHION
(RUBBER SPACER)

CUSHION CAP

LOCK NUT

HANGER PLATE

illustration **77** Truck Assembly

Truck Adjustment: When everything is in place, turn the lock nut on a few turns, then push the pivot into its socket in the hanger plate and start turning the main bolt clockwise very carefully into the threaded hole in the hanger plate. Make sure the bolt is going straight into its hole, rather than at a bad angle that will strip the threads. If there is any resistance to the turning of the main bolt, STOP turning it and find out if you are "crossing" the threads. When you have the bolt started correctly into its threads, hold onto the lock nut with your fingers and screw the main bolt all the way down (clockwise) until it is quite snug on the cushions. Try the pinky-squeeze test as in Illustration 38 to see if the bolt is tight enough. Repeat the whole process on the other truck, tighten the locknuts, then go try out your customized board. Put it through some tight, quick turns at speed. Isn't it smooooooooth? All that smoothness may be hard to get used to at first, and you may have trouble getting used to the way the board will always try to go straight for a split second after you come out of a turn, but once you are accustomed to the soft cushions you'll have to agree that they make your skateboard much more responsive, and a good deal safer at high speeds.

One problem with soft cushions is that they often wear out quickly. Boiled urethane cushions last pretty well, if they aren't over-boiled. The Bennett cushions last well too, but you may need to tighten the main bolt down on them from time to time.

Some efforts have been made to use metal springs instead of cushions on skateboard trucks. Of the two examples of metal-spring trucks I've seen, one is very erratic, especially if the spring gets twisted by accident so it is cockeyed in its socket. The other, a two-springed gadget, is pretty bulky. It seemed to work quite well if you adjusted the main bolt to your taste, but time alone will tell if it is durable.

WHEELS SHOT

Either your wheels are worn down from long hard use, or the bearing cups have broken loose in the urethane so you can't adjust them, or the bearings have gotten all rusty. You have to take off your shot wheels and put on new ones.

To replace either a sealed bearing or an open bearing wheel, just follow the directions for overhauling a wheel, as in *Crackly-grindy Bearings*, (page 139), and stick the new wheel on at the beginning of reassembly.

If you have a worn-down or ruined "precision" shielded bearing wheel, all you have to do is unscrew the axle nuts and the wheels will come off the ends of the axle; in some cases, the axle has been replaced by a bolt

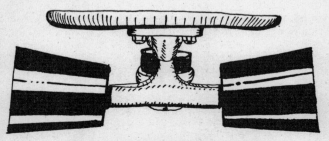

illustration **78** Coned-out Wheels

running through the truck; just loosen the nut on the end of this bolt (counter-clockwise) and remove it, then you can slide the bolt out and take the wheels off. Rather than replace the non-adjusting shielded bearing wheels with the same sort of troublesome and short-lived equipment, you should get open bearing wheels and the necessary hardware for them (see page 20 for details). You'll be happy to get bearings you can clean and adjust for better performance and longer wear. If your shielded bearing wheels were attached to the trucks by long bolts instead of axles, buy an axle that will fit the hole in the truck, and install it as in the second part of the *"Bent Axle"* procedure below. Sometimes the hole in the truck is too big for a normal 7 millimeter axle, but too small for the bigger 5/16" axle. In this case you have to get a drill and bore out the hole in the truck to 5/16" for the large axle. Put the axle into the truck according to the second half of the *"Bent Axle"* procedure.

Once you have rigged up a regular axle-set for new open bearing wheels, you can mount and adjust them as in the second half of the *"Crackly-grindy Wheels"* section above.

To avoid uneven wearing down of your wheels in the future, you can rotate them periodically; loosen the lock nut and the main bolt on each truck, then screw the bolts out and switch the front and back trucks. That way, you won't wind up with back wheels that are worn down and tiny, and front wheels that are still full-size. Different-sized wheels act differently, and when you replace one set without replacing the ones at the other end of the board, you get different degrees of traction from the new

illustration **79** Coned-out Wheels, Trucks too Tight

and the old wheels, throwing your control out of balance. So switch trucks now and then, and when all the wheels are worn down evenly, replace them all at once.

If your wheels are "coned out," or worn into cone-shapes, they are wearing down unevenly because of un-even weight distribution or overly-tightened trucks.

If the most worn-down part of each "coned-out" wheel is the inner edge (nearest to the truck as in Illustration 78), your weight is all resting on that inner edge and wearing it down, this happens frequently on wide wheels, especially if the walls of the wheel aren't tapered to the edge.

If the outer edge is more worn down than the inner edge of the wheel, it means that your main bolt is tight-ened down too much on the cushions (they're probably hard cushions, too) so the board tips up on two wheels. Loosen the main bolt a little, or replace the hard cushions with softer ones, as on page 143. Rough kick-turns will wear the outer edges of the front wheels, too. Learn to do them accurately and gingerly.

AXLE BENT

You left your skateboard in the driveway and a car ran over it. Or maybe you loaned your board to Tiny Twoton, the neighborhood heavy, and he tried to do a four foot jump, and cleared the bar, but didn't QUITE get his timing right, so he came down hard on the rear wheels. Or maybe you jumped a curb wrong and smacked the front wheels down extra hard. The result in all cases is the same; a skateboard with a bent axle that makes it ride like a Volkswagen with too many people in the back seat. The wheels hit, the steering is all whacky, and the bearings don't work right.

To replace the bent axle, first you have to get all the hardware off it and straighten it out so it can slide through the hole in the truck. Remove the wheels, as in the first part of the "Crackly-grindy Wheels" procedure on page 139. Take the inner cones off (counter-clockwise) if you can; often you can't because the bend is too sharp to let the cone loose. In this case, leave the cone where it is; you'll just strip the threads on the axle if you try to turn the cone through that bend.

When you have as much of the wheel hardware off the bent axle as you can get off, loosen (counterclockwise) the truck's lock nut and main bolt and take the truck off the skateboard so you can work on it easily. Now stick the yoke of the truck in a vise, being careful to stick it in so that the jaws grab the flat surfaces of the yoke, not the curved surfaces that might get mangled and squished by the vise. Now you have to find a couple pieces of old steel water pipe to put around the axle and straighten it. You can get them at any good hardware store or pipe supply if you can't find them lying around the house. First, get a two inch piece of ¼" I.D. (inside diameter) pipe. The pipe will actually be wider inside than that, but they still call it ¼" I.D. Cut off a half inch or a little more from one end of this little pipe and save both pieces. Slide the longer piece (it's about 1½'''long) over the end of the axle. Now get an eight inch long piece of ½" I.D. pipe and slide it over the smaller piece, as in Illustration 80. The big pipe will work as a lever so you can bend the axle back close to straight. If both ends of the axle were bent, use the same method to straighten both of them out. Check for straightness by setting the edge of a ruler across the part of the truck that the axle fits through (the axle housing); you can line up the edge of the ruler and the axle with your eye to see if your bending has gotten the axle straight enough to pull out.

You may wonder why the heck you have to take the thing out, now that you have it straight again. You could use it the way it is, but the wheels wouldn't roll right unless you got it *perfectly* straight; besides, it would bend again before long. Any metal that's been bent and re-bent is a lot weaker than it was when it was new.

Before you remove your weak axle, make sure everything has been taken off it; unscrew the cones if they were stuck on, and take the lock washers off. Then figure out which end of the axle has the knurl on it. If the truck is put into the vise as in Illustration 80, with the pivot pointing away from you, the knurl will probably be nearest to the left end, hidden just inside the axle housing part of the truck. This is the way most factories assemble their trucks. Look at the knurls on the new axle in Illustration 80 to get an idea of what they look like. Then put the short (½" long) piece of ¼" pipe over the

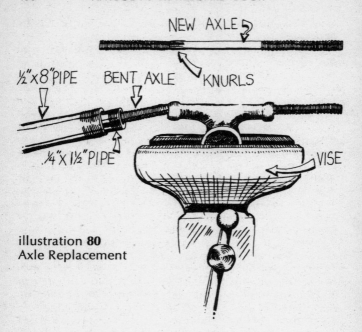

illustration **80**
Axle Replacement

left end of the axle and screw a cone onto the same end of the axle with the flat surface toward the little piece of pipe, so it will push flush against it as you turn the cone clockwise. Keep turning the cone, and it will push so hard against the little pipe that it will start to pull the axle right out of the truck. You'll see that the right end of the axle gets shorter as it is pulled through. When you have pulled about a quarter inch of the axle through, back the cone off about three turns or so (counter-clockwise), then pull the little piece of pipe away from the truck and look at the axle under there. Can you see the knurls to come out of the axle housing? If you can't see anything but a bunch of threads coming out, your axle was put into your truck by some independent-minded jackass who decided to be different from every-body else. Just spin the cone off the left end of the axle in this case, then take the ½" long piece of pipe off that end too and put it on the other end so you can pull the axle back that way until the knurls come out of the housing.

When you have turned the cone against the pipe until the knurled section of the axle is all the way out of the truck, you'll notice that it gets a lot easier to turn the cone. See if you can just push the axle the rest of the way out. If it's close to straight, it'll usually come out easily. If it's a little stuck in the truck, tap lightly on it with a hammer to get it out. Sometimes the end of the axle gets hung up inside the housing. In this case, just get a big nail or something and stick it into the truck until it hits the end of the axle, then tap on the nail with a hammer until the axle comes out. Do any tapping LIGHTLY, though. It's easy to mangle the aluminum that most trucks are made out of, and even if you don't mangle the truck, you might mash up the end of the axle so badly that it won't ever come out of the truck.

Once you have the old axle out, get a new one that's the same size and as strong as possible. You can get axles made out of all sorts of different steel alloys, each claiming to be the strongest. In fact most of the axles making the big claims aren't too much stronger than the standard cold-rolled soft steel axles; even some of the big 5/16" thick ones bend easily! In general, the axles that are black or blue-black steel are good. These axles may rust a little because they have high carbon content, but if they are heat-treated (which you can do easily to high-carbon steels) they will be very tough and bend-resistant. It's a *myth* that the shiny stainless steel axles are stronger. The only kind of stainless steel that *is* heat-treated and strong is the special, super-expensive 400 series stainless, which is used for knife blades, and which isn't completely rust-proof after all. Case-hardened soft steel is only a little better than the stainless or the un-hardened steel; the threads are stronger, but the axle will still bend easily. Cold-headed (forged) axles made of high-carbon steel can be quite a bit stronger than the cheap cold-rolled soft ones. Tracker uses the ultimate axle. It is 5/16" thick, made of 4130 chrome molybdenum steel, tempered for extra strength; it even has rolled-on threads that are stronger than the standard die-cut ones. Whew. What an effort just for an axle! But the result is almost indestructible. If you are replacing a 5/16" axle, try to get one like the Tracker axle if you can, or an axle with as many of its fine attributes. Other companies are sure to catch on and make 4130 or tool steel axles before long. There's a desperate need for strong 7 millimeter axles, especially for the radical riders who bend axles almost daily.

Whatever new axle you wind up with, slide it in from the left so the knurls wind up on the LEFT side of the truck, as in Illustration 80. Push the knurls into the housing a little by hand if you can, but DO NOT HAMMER the new axle into place. It might mash the end of the axle and mess up the threads. Just put the short (½" long) piece of little pipe on the right end of the axle, thread a cone on, and turn it clockwise until you have pulled all of the knurled section of the axle into the truck. If the knurls refuse to go into the truck because they are too big, back the cone off (counter-clockwise), then take the little pipe off and take the axle out of the truck so you can file the knurls down a little tiny bit. Slide the axle back in from the left side of the truck, put the pipe and the cone back on the right end of the axle, and pull it into place. Once the knurls have been pulled into the truck, it's hard to tell how far they've gone. To make sure you don't pull the axle in too far, measure the ends of it and keep pulling the right end until it is the same length as the left end. On most axles, this length will be about one and a quarter inches, but equalize your own axle to make sure. When you have it just right, take the cone and a piece of pipe off the left end of the axle, then put lockwashers on both axle ends and turn the inner cones into place by hand. Do both of them before you tighten either. Then tighten them both a little at a time, so you don't pull the axle one way or the other. When both cones are firmly tightened, check with a ruler to make sure the ends of the axle are of equal length, or very close to it. Then you can reassemble your wheels onto the new axle and adjust them, as on page 139, and ride away in peace. But take it easy on curbs, so you don't have to go to all the trouble of replacing your axle again for awhile.

AXLE THREADS STRIPPED

Either you tightened your axle nut too hard, or you started the nut or the cone onto the axle cockeyed, and tripped all of the threads on the end of the axle so the nut won't stay on anymore. You need a new axle, but before you can put it in, you have to get the stuff off the old one. If the nut hasn't fallen off, twist and pull it off with a socket tool and/or pliers. If the wheel was a sealed bearing one, just pull it off, cut the stripped tip of the axle off with a hacksaw, and go to the third paragraph of "Axle Bent" to get your axle out. If the wheel is an open bearing one, take a socket tool that fits the cone snugly (see Illustration 15) and put it on the cone that's still on the axle. Turn the cone (counter-clockwise) right through the stripped section of threads, making sure you don't push on the socket tool as if you were trying to screw the cone on instead of off. It takes a gentle touch, or the cone will just strip out too. If you twist the cone out without pushing it at all, you'll be able to make new threads with it and get it off the axle. But don't use the axle with these halfway threads. Use the procedures under "Axle Bent," above. Pull the axle out from the UNSTRIPPED END, not which side the knurls are on; if you try to use those weak threads to pull the axle, they'll just strip out all over again. Put a new axle in, and next time BE MORE CAREFUL as you start cones and nuts onto the axle and then tighten them down.

WHEELS HITTING

You pinched and scrimped and saved up your pennies and finally bought a set of those snazzy great big wheels all the hot-shot skaters have been talking about; but now that you've put them on your trucks, you find that every time you do a hot turn, the big wheels rub on the bottom of your board.

There are three separate remedies for your lack of wheel clearance; you can put the board up higher on risers on special high trucks, or you can gouge out channels for your wheels in the underside of the board, or you can give up those snazzy big wheels for good smaller ones that don't rub. You might even want to try a combination of a couple of the possible solutions, like risers *and* channeling.

The cheapest and simplest thing to do is to unscrew all the machine screws or whatever's holding your trucks to the board top, then put in ¼" or ½" riser pads, so the board will be raised up above the wheels more. But many people find that the higher the board is, the harder it is to do quick turns, and the easier it is to slide when you get into a good hard turn. The geometry behind these difficulties is pretty complicated, but it's basically due to leverage. If you raise yourself and the board up higher above the wheels, you have to move around more to make the wheels pivot. Also your weight shoves with more leverage from the side in turns, thus making it easier to slide. Some skateboarders don't mind being up high; once they get used to it, especially on big boards, they use the high position to advantage, developing strong, radical styles with big movement and lots of body english. But if you liked your board the way it was before the wheels started hitting, you should put on risers that are as small as possible, like ¼" if you can get away with it. There are risers made out of a variety of materials, including soft rubber, polypropelene, Lexan, urethane, birch plywood, and aluminum. If you want a firm feel to your board, like for freestyle, get hard risers, like those of Lexan, birch, or aluminum. If you want the risers to absorb shocks, like if you ride a fiberglass board on rough pavement, you can use birch plywood (it absorbs shocks in its many layers of wood) or urethane, or the soft rubber risers. The trouble with soft rubber risers, though, is that they squish out of shape with use so the screws can come loose.

A homemade solution to the riser problem is to cut your own risers out of the sidewalls of old car tires. Use a supersharp utility razor knife carefully, and cut out pieces of tire that are a little bigger than your hanger plates. Then put them in place on the bottom of the board, drill the holes through from the deck side, and attach your trucks again. These tire risers will absorb lots of shock, but won't squish around and loosen up on you.

For a much higher cost, you can solve your wheel clearance problem with specially designed high trucks like the Bennett Hijackers. They will work with most wheels, and are very sensitive for fast turns or freestyle work. But they cost. Brewer trucks are high too, but have standard turning geometry and are more reasonably priced.

If you still have trouble with your wheels hitting now

and then, even after you have put risers or good trucks on your board, you can cut wheel channels into the underside of the board, using a Surform tool on a drill as in Illustration 51. Wear safety glasses when you do this job, and if you're cutting into fiberglass, wear a cloth or dust-mask over your mouth and nose, and gloves and long sleeves over your hands and arms; the Surform tool kicks up a lot of glass dust when it is being used on a fiberglass board, and that glass dust is itchy, *ornery* stuff when its gets into your skin or inside you.

Some people worry about whether wheel channels weaken the board. I don't think they weaken any board that is structurally sound in the first place. If it is a thick hardwood board, or a thin hardwood board built like the one with the birch plywood plates on page 85, the channels won't hurt anything unless you carve them in much farther than is necessary.

Fiberglass boards will hold up even after radical channeling. Pine boards may be a little weaker if you cut deep channels into them, but if you split your pine board, it won't cost you much time and effort to replace it.

If all else fails, you may have to give up your snazzy big wheels. This may seem like a let-down, but you can put on snazzy *smaller* wheels like the small Road Riders or the Roller Sports slicks and do almost anything you need, just at a lower rate of speed.

TRUCKS OR BOARD TOP CRACKING

You may notice a creaky-cracking sound when you ride your board. Or you may be looking at your truck and see a little hairline crack somewhere around the socket for the pivot. If you notice either of these warning signs, DON'T RIDE THE BOARD!!!! Heed the warning. If the board is cracking, it might be about to break, and it won't break when you aren't using it. It'll break when you really torque on it, and then you'll fall, and maybe a part of *you* will break as well as the board. Before this happens, replace the board with a strong new one. Look through the equipment section of the chapter on whatever type of riding you do, so you get a board that's made for what you want to do with it. That way you won't do any more board-and-body breaking.

If you have a cracked hanger plate, you can usually buy a replacement without having to buy a whole new truck. If the shop where you get your skateboard equipment doesn't have the exact same kind of hanger plate that you broke, you may be able to use another brand that's interchangeable. Just take the truck and main bolt from your board to the shop and see if they fit well. Don't try to use any combination of parts that doesn't go together easily. If the main bolt from your truck doesn't fit the new hanger, just substitute the main bolt that's supposed to go with the plate. If you can't get your old parts and the available new parts together, or if you break off a truck yoke instead of a hanger plate, you have to get a whole new truck, then promise yourself to take it a little easier jumping curbs and jamming through harsh drainage ditch deflections.

HANGER PLATE THREADS STRIPPED

You started the main bolt in at an angle and it got cross-threaded, or you pulled the truck off the hanger plate before the bolt was all the way loose, or you let the lock nut and the main bolt work loose as you were riding and the main bolt finally just stripped out of its hole. The result of any of the above mistakes is that the inside of the main bolt hole in the hanger doesn't have any threads left in it. You have to replace the hanger plate. When you have your new hanger plate attached to the board, BE CAREFUL as you start the main bolt into its threads. Make sure it is going straight in; loosen the lock nut and wiggle the cushions around on the main bolt so the bolt has room to move freely in the yoke. When the bolt is adjusted the way you want it, make sure you lock the nut against the hanger plate so the whole outfit can't come loose and strip out again.

TAIL DRAGGING, NOSE BASHING

If you do freestyle stunts or radical riding with a lot of kick-turns, you tend to wear down the back end of your board where it hits the pavement. If you are a freestyle specialist, you should keep in mind that competition judges usually dock points for tail dragging; try to learn

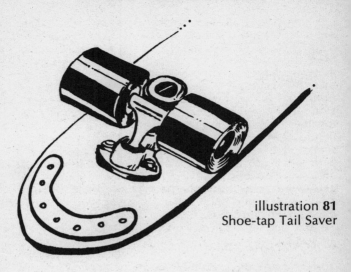

illustration **81**
Shoe-tap Tail Saver

how to do all your kick-turns and rotation stunts *without* letting the tail (or nose) of the board hit the ground. But if you don't care for competition, or if you're just a radical rider who likes to set that old tail down on a steep bank and crank the board around, like Ben Marcus is doing on the back cover, you're going to wear either your shoe or the tail of the board down.

For worn-down shoes there's this magic stuff called Shoe-goo that you build up on the sole of the shoe where you need it. You can get Shoe-goo at big shoe stores and shoe repair shops, or you can look at sport shops that cater to runners and tennis players.

For worn down tail-ends of skateboards they haven't invented anything like Shoe-goo yet. One solution to the problem is to get a kick-tail board; they make it easier to do kickturns without dragging. If you can't afford a kick-tail board, you might be able to get a tail plate made of steel that'll fit your board, or you might just get an aluminum board. The trouble with any metal-tailed board, though, is that it will still wear down, and when it does, the edge will get sharp and cut you if you touch it. For this problem, you have to take a fine-grade metal

illustration **82**
Wood Tail Saver

file and smooth down the sharp edge. Make even filing
strokes that wrap around the edge so they round it off.

If you have a wood board, you can attach a steel heel
tap tail-saver to it, as in Illustration 81. Use Barge cement
and tacks or tiny screws to hold the tap in place. Some
big-board riders like Tom Sims attach blocks of hardwood
such as hard rock maple to the tails of their boards.
Shape the block like the one in Illustration 82, then attach
it to the board with strong glue (Elmer's or Titebond
aliphatic resin) and flathead screws coming through the
board from the deck.

Kevin Reed invented a radical solution to the tail-
dragging problem, one which works very well and gives
you a neat foot rest like a kick-tail. Get an old main bolt
from a discarded truck, and one of the hard cushions
and the old lock nut as well. Then go to a hardware store
and buy a couple of big fender washers that will fit
around the main bolt. The wider and the thicker these
washers are, the better. Then get a little thin washer that
goes around the main bolt, one that is less than ¾" wide.
Put one of the big fender washers in place on the tail of
the board so its edges are just sticking out beyond the
edge of the tail, then drill the hole for the main bolt
through the board. Arrange all the hardware around the
bolt as shown in Illustration 83, and tighten the bolt hard,
so it squishes the cushion down and bulges its sides out.
If the bolt sticks down so far that it hits the pavement

before the fender washers do, you can either leave it and let it wear down, or cut it off near the nut.' The great thing about this tail-saver is that it's cheap and easy to replace. Also, it makes a nice little foot-rest for your back foot when you want to do kick-turns, three-sixties, and stuff like that. If you skateboard at night some time (not generally recommended unless you know the pavement is clean and smooth) do some tail-dragging and watch the sparks that the bolt and/or washers make when they hit the concrete. Whoopie! Just don't use this device on the smooth walls of swimming pools. It tends to make big ugly marks.

For nose bashing you can use the tail-saving devices, or (on a wood board) just take a short piece of fan belt and nail it around the nose for collision protection. Wood boards need something up there to keep from being split.

BOARD CHIPPED OR SPLINTERY

If you're in the slam-bang school of skateboarding, and you have a board made of either fiberglass or wood, the rails will get fractured, dinged, and battered. Splinters of glass or wood from these rough places can cut you; fiberglass can make a really mean abrasion if you hit it wrong, and wood splinters are no fun, especially if you pick them up while sitting on the board.

The solution for a sharp-edged or splintery board is the same, whether it's a fiberglass or a wood board. Take a file to the especially rough places, and then use medium grade sandpaper to round and smooth things down so there's nothing left to cut or jab you.

MAIN BOLT HITTING

When you go through a deflection or over a bump or over a big crack in the sidewalk, the head of your main bolt hits the ground. There are three different solutions to this problem. You can get new and larger diameter wheels. Or you can get soft cushions and tighten your main bolt more. Or, if you don't have any money for the two solutions above, you can take your cushions off the main bolt (see page 143), then cut about 1/4" off one of them. When you reassemble the truck, put this thin extra

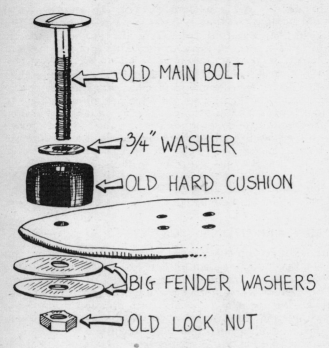

OLD MAIN BOLT

3/4" WASHER

OLD HARD CUSHION

BIG FENDER WASHERS

OLD LOCK NUT

illustration **83** Kevin's Tail Saver

piece of cushion right next to the regular-size cushion, which goes nearest to the hanger plate. The new cut-down cushion should go between the head of the main bolt and the yoke, thus allowing the main bolt to move up higher off the ground. Also, go over cracks in concrete *diagonally* from now on; that will keep the bolt head up.

9
History of The Wheel

All this bull about when skateboarding started has got to be straightened out. The following is the definitive history of the ultimate personal vehicle.

First there was the Stone Age. That was a bad time. Long before urethane. Before clay wheels were invented, even. People with coned-out heads went around hitting each other and throwing rocks and making odd little piles out of the bones of their enemies, piles that archaeologists have dug up and wondered about endlessly. The bone-studiers keep asking each other "why did these stony people have so many broken elbows?"

Any skateboarder can tell you the answer to that one. Those guys with the coned-out heads probably saw a big Stone Age pebble rolling down a hill one day, and started trying to ride it. It must have been pretty tricky, what with the poor traction of stone and no pavement around. It was probably a big fad for a while, nonetheless. Stunt stone riders had exhibitions, young daredevils rode avalanches, and parents probably refused to let their kids bring their pet stones into the cave. But there must have been a lot of bad falls and broken elbows, because the fad died out.

Following the Stone Age, after a long period of time during which people didn't have much to do other than learning how to farm and how to invent religions, there was a Bronze Age. This was a pretty classy age. They made shiny skateboards and emblazoned them with sapphires and the names of hot-shot riders like Ty Tutankhamen and Imhotep Weaver. But the boards lost their flex after awhile, and a lot of the skateboarders got arrested for skating down sacred tombstones, and once again, the thrill went out of it. Most of the big dealers went back to rugs and photographs for tourists.

There was a brief and glorious Wood Age, during which designers found out that they could build all shapes and sizes of boards out of this wonderful material, but the designers got carried away and tried to use wood for the wheels as well as the board tops. Wood wheels worked, and were inexpensive, but they didn't last long enough to make skateboarding a practical sport. Discus and Javelin throwing still drew the big crowds.

Not long after the Wood Age there was a long Dark Age, during which people fought off plagues, or busied themselves with conquering their near and far neighbors when they were healthy. Roads had been built, but the surfaces were still too rough. A few die-hards hung on all the way through that period, but they were ignored by the ignorant masses.

Then there was the Iron Age. It filled men's heads with ideas and filled the air with smoke. One of the last and clearest ideas of the Iron Age was the roller skate wheel. This was followed soon after by the invention of the adjustable clamp-on skate that could fit any shoe. Very soon after this some unknown kid found out that you could take a clamp-on skate apart, nail the two ends to a board, and go coasting down hills. The skateboard thus produced worked pretty well, and could even be steered a little, especially if you put a box and a steering pole at the front end. Kids could be seen riding down paved hills all over the civilized world. But the metal wheels were loud and slippery in corners and hard on the nerves. And if you ever hit a pebble or anything, they stopped dead and sent you flying over or through the steering pole. So even though some kids kept using the Iron Age skateboards for some time, it never got much beyond the neighborhood hillside.

Then there was the Clay Age. Archaeologists don't say too much about this period; many of them don't even realize that the Clay Age stretched all the way up to about 1972, when skateboards were still using ceramic composition wheels. During the height of the Clay Age, about 1965,

there were millions of skateboarders all over America, using the mostly wood and clay and iron equipment that had been handed down from previous ages. The trucks on these 1965 boards were more developed, and people appreciated the quick turns they could make with their Sure Grip equipped boards, but NOBODY who was into skateboarding liked the fact that whenever you cranked too hard into a sharp turn, your wheels spun out and dumped you on the ground. Too many people wound up on the ground due to the ceramic wheels; the fad died once again, and the field of skateboarding was left to the die-hards, who either made do with clay, or used rubber composition wheels and wore out a set about every other week.

Then, in about 1972 or 1973, there was for skateboarding the dawn of the greatest period, the Plastic Age. And

many who had scoffed and spat upon the shiny dispos-
able see-through sanitary metal-flaked useless products
of the plastic industries were forced to admit that at
last, something of real worth had been invented. It was
the urethane wheel. At last, there was a wheel that did
not stop at every pebble like the old steel wheels, and
that did *not* go into a slide the second you tried to turn
sharply on it, and that didn't wear down nearly as fast as
its predecessors. It seemed like magic; Frank Nasworthy
was the magician.

Of course, there were problems at first. The bearing
cups had a habit of popping loose on the early urethane
wheels, for one thing. And when manufacturers made the
wheels hard enough to keep the bearing cups in place,
they were a little too skittery. But not for long. Soon
better grades and formulae for urethane were tried out,
and the Stoker appeared. Although many riders did not
like that name, they all had to admit that it *was* a Stoke
to ride a skateboard with those big road-gripping wheels.
And then the sealed bearing Road Rider wheels appeared
in all their silent magically gripping splendor. Skateboarding became not just a kid's past-time, but a full grown
SPORT.

The plastics industry obliged by producing strong,
resilient, fiberglass boards, and reliable and cheap Lexan
and polypropelene boards as well, and such marvels as
Mr. Bennett's wonderful Red Rubber cushions. New
trucks with improved design and materials came along
too, allowing skateboarders to take on challenges they
never would have dreamed possible a few years before.
There are now so many things to do on a skateboard it's
hard to decide which to try first. Cities and towns have
even begun to make public skateboard parks for the
delight of the local enthusiasts.

But what of the future? Will the Plastic Age of skateboards fade amid a flood of injuries, as all the other
fads have? I hope not. I hope more skateboarders will
take to wearing padding and helmets, and I hope that
public agencies provide good parks for the practice of
this great sport, and I hope that competition remains
healthy, be it backyard or Olympic. And I hope that
whoever you are, if you are into skateboarding, you will
try to do what's fun for *you* to do on *your* board, so

the sport can go on being as variegated as the people who enjoy it.

I like to think that there might be a long-lasting Laminate Age, with not only the ingenious laminations of skateboard materials from previous periods, but also the coexistence of widely diverse styles, techniques and terrains so that *all* kinds of people can find facets of the sport that turn them on.

Index

Bantam Book Catalog

It lists over a thousand money-saving best-sellers originally priced from $3.75 to $15.00 —bestsellers that are yours now for as little as 60¢ to $2.95!

The catalog gives you a great opportunity to build your own private library at huge savings!

So don't delay any longer—send us your name and address and 25¢ (to help defray postage and handling costs).